THE SMALL GREENHOUSE

Small Garden Series

Editor: C. E. Lucas Phillips

THE SMALL GREENHOUSE

H. G. WITHAM FOGG

A PAN ORIGINAL

Revised edition

PAN BOOKS LTD : LONDON

First published 1965 by

PAN BOOKS LTD

33 Tothill Street, London, S.W.1

ISBN 0 330 23089 1

2nd (Revised) Printing 1972
3rd Printing 1973

Printed in Great Britain by
Cox & Wyman Ltd, London, Reading and Fakenham

CONTENTS

ILLUSTRATIONS IN COLOUR
(between pages 72 and 73)

IN BLACK AND WHITE
(between pages 64 and 65)

LINE DRAWINGS

CHAPTER I

INTRODUCING THE GREENHOUSE

Who loves a garden loves a greenhouse too,
Unconscious of a less propitious clime,
There blooms exotic beauty, warm and snug,
While the winds whistle and the snows descend.

I MAKE NO APOLOGY for quoting Cowper's well-known lines, for they sum up so aptly the benefits of what might be called weather-proof gardening.

Most people start their gardening activities without a greenhouse, but soon learn the handicaps they work under and the opportunities that are closed to them. The greenhouse vastly enlarges the scope of one's gardening, saves the costs of buying many kinds of plants, enables one to propagate one's chosen sorts, provides plants to adorn the house in winter and enables one to work comfortably in shirt sleeves 'while the winds whistle and the snows descend'.

On the other hand, unless one indulges in a completely automatic structure, with everything controlled electrically, a greenhouse cannot take care of itself. If a mixed bag of plants is grown, it will need some attention every day. Maybe that may mean nothing more than opening and shutting the ventilators, but the point I wish to make is that the greenhouse, unlike the celebrated sparking plug, is not a case of 'fit and forget'. Thus, if you go off on holiday for two or three weeks in August, you will find the tomatoes at death's door unless you have provided them with a foster-nurse.

Therefore, you must decide in advance, in broad terms, what you want the greenhouse for. You may, of course, change your intent later, but there is no communism in the greenhouse and there has to be some segregation and selection right from the start. To a very large extent, this selection will be determined by the amount of heating you can afford to provide. In this respect houses are classified as 'cold', 'cool', 'warm' or 'hot'.

A **'cold'** house is one with no heating at all. It can be used only for plants that will stand a low temperature and a certain amount of frost. It will accommodate vines (which benefit from a freeze), hardy bulbs, such as daffodils and tulips, and the seedlings or dormant roots of other hardy plants. The great drawback to the cold house is that it admits not only cold air but also damp air and fog, at a time when damp is liable to be most injurious.

The **'cool'** house is one which is heated just a little more than enough to keep it frost-proof, maintaining a minimum temperature of 42°. Here the way at once opens up. Much can be done. Not only can many tender plants be brought safely through till next spring, such as pelargoniums ('geraniums'), azaleas, carnations – but also winter floral displays can be enjoyed from spring-flowering bulbs, cinerarias, schizanthus and several primulas (*P. malacoides, P. obconica* and *P. kewensis*). The cool house is also excellent for growing annuals for early bloom. Indeed, with good planning, the cool house can give a colourful display throughout the year.

The **'warm'** greenhouse is one in which the temperature always remains above 55°. It allows an even wider and more interesting range of plants to be cultivated. In such a house, apart from ornamental subjects, many vegetables and certain fruits can be brought to maturity much earlier than they can outdoors and at a time when they are expensive to buy.

The **'hot'** house is one in which the heating system is capable of maintaining a temperature of between 70° and 75° and is therefore most suitable for forcing and for growing tropical plants.

Accordingly, greenhouse and plant must match each other. Thus, if your main interest is in chrysanthemums or tomatoes on the one hand or in such tropical luxuries as poinsettias or gerberas on the other, further occupants of the greenhouse, if any, must be chosen from among plants that like approximately the same conditions. For example, the popular zonal pelargoniums, *Primula sinensis*, and forced bulbs to bloom in winter need a night temperature of 50°; gloxinias, Lorraine begonias and other tropicals must have 65° throughout the winter. Of course, if your purse permits, you may buy a long enough structure which can be divided into cool, warm and hot houses at will.

Probably the best advice to give to those with little experience is to start with a cool house and with simple plants.

In all these matters, bear in mind that it is the *night* temperature that is important. A sudden fall in the temperature of the outside air may be very damaging and provision must be made accordingly in the supply of heat and the cotting of thermostats. Throughout this book temperatures are given in Fahrenheit.

CHAPTER II

GREENHOUSES AND THEIR EQUIPMENT

TYPES – WOODEN FRAMEWORKS – METAL AND
CONCRETE – GLASS SUBSTITUTES – SITING –
FOUNDATIONS – EQUIPMENT – THE POTTING
SHED – FRAMES

THERE ARE THREE standard styles of greenhouse – the 'span' or 'ridge', the 'three-quarter span' and the 'lean-to'.

The span is a complete and independent structure, with a ridged roof, standing in splendid isolation. For all-round purposes, it is the best.

The lean-to is simply half a greenhouse built against a wall.

The three-quarter span is just what it says, but also built up against a wall. It is a very good type of greenhouse, providing the right sort of ventilation.

The glazed porches attached to many houses are also a sort of greenhouse. Their fault, as a rule, is that, though there is often a draught, there is no proper top ventilation.

'Dutch lights' are very large sheets of glass (about 56 in. by 28 in.) held in light wooden frameworks, originally intended for use in garden frames. Complete greenhouses are now made with them. They are particularly useful for crops that are to be grown in the soil of the greenhouse (the 'greenhouse border') rather than in pots, as, for example, vines, tomatoes and other vegetables, chrysanthemums, carnations; but staging can be erected in them for pot plants also. They have the advantages of being cheaper than the traditional types and of admitting maximum light, but needing more heat in winter and being subject to sharp fluctuations of temperature in summer. Also they are very vulnerable to the projectiles of small boys.

For general horticultural use, the traditional style of greenhouse, having low walls of brick, concrete or wood, still has many advantages. It preserves heat, particularly in winter, and is not subject to the same violent changes as the all-glass-house. Many of the plants that we shall have to consider object to very strong sunlight and, in any type of house, require to be shaded.

New ideas are constantly being introduced into the design and the materials of greenhouses, so that glass seems to be the only constant item. Even for glass, a substitute in the form of plastic is sometimes employed, but this can be regarded as of only temporary value.

Wooden Frameworks

Although cost is bound to be a major factor in deciding the type of house to be bought, another important question to answer is whether it should be of wood or metal. Both have their advantages. A point worth remembering is that, to a man who does his own repairs, wood presents no difficulty, while the fitting of shelves and other requirements is easier where wood is used.

The type of wood to be used for the framework presents the usual problem of value for money. Teak is both strong and very durable but it is also expensive. The wood generally known as red deal or redwood, and sometimes as yellow deal, is very largely used in the best modern structures. It comes from *Pinus sylvestris*, the Scotch Pine.

While not so strong as teak, it is very reliable and has the advantage of easier working, although the softer, paler outer wood should be rejected, since it has little durability. It is the yellowish-red heartwood which should be used, to avoid materials having twisted grain and many knots.

The ordinary white deal, which comes from *Picea excelsa*, and pine from the Douglas fir, are best avoided, for they have little weather resistance and are inclined to split. When available, the so-called Pitch Pine wood from *Pinus palustris*, can be used along the guttering, since it is very resistant to water injury.

The 'Western red cedar' is obtained from *Thuya plicata* and is most durable, resisting the penetration of moisture which is the chief cause of decay. It is cheaper than teak. This wood is sometimes used unpainted, but it should then be dressed with linseed oil from time to time, in order to give protection from decay and to counteract the increase in porosity which occurs as the wood ages.

Oak is durable but expensive, but when used in conjunction with a steel framework the cost is lessened. This has been done with great success by one of the leading greenhouse manufacturers. Oak should be straight grained, otherwise it is inclined to become distorted.

Wood therefore can be summed up under three headings:

Very durable – teak, western red cedar, oak.
Durable   – long-leaf pitch-pine.
Not durable – Norway spruce or 'white wood'.

The life of the woodwork can be greatly prolonged by treating it with a preservative. Apart from linseed oil, which should be used on teak and red cedar, all other woods should be safeguarded against premature rotting. There are several proprietary water solution preservatives, which are both easy to apply and quite effective. Do NOT use creosote, excepting for any wood which is actually buried in the soil. Creosote gives off fumes which are very harmful to plant life and continues to do so for a long period after the wood has been treated.

White lead paint helps to preserve the wood and reflects light. There are also special paints available for use on the ironwork and hinges.

Metal and Concrete

Metal greenhouses have been developed during the last fifteen years. It was largely due to the very great difficulty in obtaining suitable timber after the 1939–45 War that they became widely used.

Both steel and aluminium alloys are used. In some respects, the former is less popular, since, generally speaking, it cannot be used for shaping in the same way as the aluminium. Some steel is, of course, frequently used in timber greenhouses, including some parts of the ventilators and for the purlin posts.

Aluminium alloys are being used most successfully for the making of houses of all sizes. Pure aluminium would be useless, since it is soft, but the addition of small amounts of other metals forms an alloy of great strength.

Although they lack the elegance of wood or metal, concrete houses are used on quite a substantial scale, chiefly by commercial growers. Here again, their invention is largely due to the post-war shortage of timber. Reinforced with wire rods, concrete becomes both strong and durable.

Whichever style of greenhouse you elect to have, try, if you can, to inspect a model before buying. Many of the mass-produced houses offered, especially those of a wooden framework, are of indifferent materials and slovenly manufacture, with ill-fitting joints and with doors and windows that do not shut properly. Beware, therefore, of the 'Cheap line'. All greenhouses should be so made that they can be shut tightly – a requisite that is particularly important when the house has to be fumigated against pests. Metal greenhouses with sliding doors are suspect on this account.

Another common failing of 'popular' small greenhouses is that they are fitted with insufficient ventilation, particularly overhead ventilation along the ridge, which is of capital importance.

Glass Substitutes

During the last few years prominence has been given to the use of plastic as an alternative to glass. However, even on price alone, no plastic sheeting will be able to compete with glass in the long run, not even if it is made scratch-proof and easy to cut.

This does not mean that plastic cannot be used on certain occasions, for sometimes it will serve as an alternative to glass. Polyethylene, better known as polythene, is translucent and, although it is offered under specific trade names, it is more or less a standardized product. This material needs renewing at fairly frequent intervals since it is affected by continued bright sunlight. Although it does not break in the same way as glass, it is liable to be damaged, so that there is not much to choose between glass and polythene in this respect.

Another form of plastic sheeting is known technically as Polyvinyl-chloride or P.V.C. This is transparent and less flexible than polythene. Its brittleness varies according to the additions made in its manufacture.

Plastic houses are very suitable for providing protection for various plants during the summer and early autumn months, but they cannot be regarded as anything more than temporary structures.

Glass is easier to clean, for so often dirt accumulates and moisture condenses on plastics resulting in a great reduction in the quality of light transmitted. This is true even with brands of polythene which have been treated to minimize this possibility. Glass, therefore, is the only safe bet for permanency; get a good horticultural grade, free of bubbles and undulations.

Plastic is of value for covering plants which need shading from time to time during the summer. It also gives protection from rain, draughts and winds, and is of value as an inner lining for a cold greenhouse, preventing the temperature from falling very low at night.

Siting

The siting of the greenhouse is of great importance, but may sometimes be in part influenced by the nature of one's property. For a few specialist purposes, as in the Victorian ferneries, a lean-to on the northern side of the house may be best. In general, however, full sun exposure is of the first importance – not in the shadow of trees or buildings from east, south or west. On the other hand, it is best not exposed to strong winds, especially from the north or east, which will cause loss of heat and probable draughts. Bear in mind, however, that, although a sunny place is needed, artificial shading will be needed for some plants in high summer.

The traditional alignment for a greenhouse is north-and-south, but many good authorities now prefer it east-and-west, on the ground that it improves the transmission of light.

Foundations

For every type of permanent glasshouse proper foundations are of paramount importance. Most greenhouse makers will supply a ground plan to which it is necessary to adhere, if the job of laying the foundation is to be entirely satisfactory. Various materials are used for the purpose.

A simple foundation can be made by taking out a trench of the right depth, keeping the sides vertical. A wedge of concrete, at least a foot wide and 4 to 5 in. deep, is made and on this is built the brick footing. If the base of the greenhouse is to be of brickwork, several layers of bricks are used. Alternatively, concrete blocks, including the cavity type, can be used both for the footings and walls.

Provision for the proper getaway of water and good surrounds to the greenhouse are other important considerations at the time the greenhouse is being erected. A hard approach path is essential since the house will have to be visited regularly in all weathers. It can be a utilitarian one of concrete or a more decorative one of stone or brick.

Greenhouse Equipment

Having considered the shell of the house and its footings, we must now look briefly at its furniture and fittings.

Since rainwater is so necessary for many plants and since, for all, water of the greenhouse temperature is vastly superior to stone-cold water from a tap, especially in winter, it is astonishing how often people forget to make the simple provisions necessary for it. These consist merely in fitting guttering to the eaves and a pipe or pipes leading to a tank fitted inside the house. Fit also an overflow to the outside, leading either to the dwelling-house system (not the drains) or to a sump-pit or ditch, etc. Fit the tank itself with a wooden lid, to prevent things from falling into it and to discourage enterprising youth from experimental exercises.

On the floor of the house, normally along the centre line, a path is necessary. This should be of concrete or of non-slip tiles. Stone and brick paths are apt to become slippery unless treated in winter with the 'tar-oil wash' used on fruit trees.

On either side of this path, staging may or may not be required. It will not be needed if your intention is to grow plants at ground level in a border of soil. Such soil borders should always be left, even if staging for pot plants is to be fixed, as, when dampened, they help to create the humidity necessary for most plants in hot weather. To damp down a concrete expanse is not sufficient.

Staging may also be of several sorts. In a span greenhouse it will normally be on both sides of the central path. In the three-quarter or the lean-to, it is often preferred, for display purposes, to have tiers of stepped-back staging on one side of the house only (in which case the path will be along the side of the house at the foot of the staging).

The usual slatted staging is adequate for simple purposes, but not ideal. It tends to be dry and draughty. A better plan is to convert the bench into a large, shallow trough, about 2 in. deep and filled to a depth of at least an inch with small pebbles, breeze, or weathered ashes, which are kept uniformly moist. Such trays are on the market in fibre-glass or galvanized iron, or they may be home-made.

Most gardeners will certainly want to raise seedlings and for this purpose one or more shelves will need to be fitted high up a foot or so from the roof, so that they get maximum light and do not become 'drawn' and leggy.

FIG. 1. Metal Greenhouse Staging with shelf for seedlings

A maximum-and-minimum thermometer will be needed and another probable requirement is a propagating frame, which I shall discuss later. The tools wanted are few: a good syringe, a trowel, a fine-rosed watering can, $\frac{1}{4}$-in. and $\frac{1}{2}$-in.

sieves, and one or more 'potting sticks' which are flat sticks an inch wide for ramming soil down into pots; one will need to be $\frac{1}{4}$ in. thick and another $\frac{1}{2}$ in.

The Potting Shed

A necessary adjunct of the greenhouse is a small well-lit shed for sowing, transplanting and potting. This may well be done in the greenhouse, but a separate shed is more convenient and makes for better hygiene in the greenhouse, and the growing and displaying of plants. The separate structure can also be used to house tools and equipment.

Very often the potting shed can adjoin the glasshouse, making it easy for the taking in and out of the plants being pricked off and potted up. A potting shed ensures that potting soils do not remain icy cold and plants escape chills which they sometimes sustain through standing in cold places while waiting to be pricked off or potted up. Flower-pots can be kept under cover which will keep them from frost damage and prevent green algae from gaining a hold, a point often overlooked.

A shed with good sized windows, a firm, solid bench, and suitable racks for the storage of pot boxes and pots, is ideal. A few containers for holding potting mixtures and the separate ingredients ensures that these are kept clean.

The Frame

The garden frame or 'light' is the lady-in-waiting of the greenhouse and should be placed in close attendance at the feet of its mistress. It is a greenhouse in miniature and has many uses – to raise plants from cuttings, to 'harden off' young non-hardy plants which have been grown from seed in the greenhouse (such as antirrhinums, zinnias, asters, petunias), for over-wintering and for raising early vegetable crops on the 'hot bed' system.

The body of the frame may be made from brick, breeze

blocks, wood or metal; portable frames of metal or wood are also very handy.

The size of the English 'light' is 6 ft by 4 ft. It is divided with $1\frac{1}{4}$-in. sash bars into four sections, each of which is glazed with four panes of glass overlapping, each being 18 in. by 12 in. There are several variations of this size, and, where a lighter structure is required, the so-called 'Ladies Light' can be used. This measures 4 ft by 3 ft, and the timber used is much lighter than that of the normal English frame. One disadvantage of the normal English light, is that, because of its construction and the thickness of wood used, the maximum amount of sunshine is prevented from reaching the plants.

The Dutch light, of which I have already spoken, has now come into favour. The glass slips into grooves in the sides and is held in place by wooden stops at each end. The drawback here is that, if the glass gets broken, it has to be replaced in its entirety and not, as in the case of the English light, by a single pane.

There is a smaller structure often known as the French light, although it is not generally available in this country. It is not difficult to make, and measures 4 ft 4 in. wide by 4 ft 5 in. long. The sides and top are made of 2 in. $\times$ 2 in. wood. There are three sash bars, and the glass needed consists of twelve panes, each 14 in. $\times$ 12 in. and four panes of 8 in. $\times$ 12 in. Putty is required only at the top of the frame.

There are many first-class garden frames offered by the leading manufacturers today. These include the wooden frames, and the rustless sectional frames of cast aluminium. As far as wooden frames are concerned, there are many types available, but undoubtedly cedar wood, although more expensive than other woods, is the most reliable. It is durable and requires the minimum of upkeep.

The value of the frame is vastly increased if it can be heated. This can be done inexpensively by a very small paraffin stove, but electricity is much to be preferred. I deal briefly with this method in the next chapter.

Since the frame is a greenhouse in miniature, its management is governed by similar rules, which I outline in Chapter IV. Ventilation is of great importance. The general aim should be to give it as much as the weather will allow. This is done by lifting (*not* sliding) the light, either to its fullest extent in fine, warm weather, or propped open a mere inch or so when it is cold, and of course completely closed on frosty days and nights. Open it always in a direction away from the wind. For really tough weather, Archangel mats or thick sacking should be spread over the top, but a little ventilation should be given occasionally if *air* heating has been installed (see next Chapter).

CHAPTER III

HEATING

THE OLD-FASHIONED method of heating greenhouses by large hot-water pipes from outside boilers fired by coal, coke, or, more recently, oil or gas, is probably still the most efficient. It is not, however, one that most amateurs are likely to choose today for small structures; certainly not coal or coke boilers, which drag you out on chilly nights. People who inherit these solid fuel boilers from previous owners can now have them changed to the uses of oil by a conversion unit or, more expensively, can convert them to electricity.

What the modern man is more likely to go for is either the paraffin stove or electricity.

Paraffin Stoves

Paraffin is far and away the cheaper to install (though doubtfully cheaper to run) and it is quite suitable for very small structures. But it has several disadvantages. The stove must be filled every day or every other day; the heat is not very well distributed, so that there are cold corners in the house; and the volume of heat cannot be controlled to suit particular plants or to counteract sudden low or high changes in the outer air. However, a great many people get very good results this way and it may be the only way open to many pockets. In fact, a paraffin stove is a very good stand-by in the event of those electrical failures or stoppages which are by no means unknown even in this allegedly progressive age.

If opting for an oil stove, choose a blue-flame burner rather than a yellow-flame one and choose one that heats up a little water, to provide a degree of humidity.

Electricity

We come, therefore, to electricity, and here we enter into a technical field in which a certain amount of specialist knowledge is needed (more than you might think). All I can do here is to generalize and to advise you to consult a specialist for your particular case, unless you happen to be one yourself. The Electrical Association of Savoy Hill, London, WC2, which is a non-trading advisory service run by the industry, publishes a useful booklet called *Electricity in Your Garden* and a most valuable guide it is. Manufacturers of electrical equipment will also be helpful. In any event, people who are not well up in these things should have the equipment installed by a qualified electrician, who will connect up with the dwelling-house main. It is vital that all equipment should be safe – waterproof, proof against chemical sprays and earthed – and that it should be fitted by a man who knows his business.

Electricity is the most expensive but the least troublesome form of heating. There is no going out at 'chilly dawn or eve' to stoke or trim. With a waterproof thermostat of the rod type fitted and properly set, one has little to do on the score of heat but to pay the bills, which are not serious for a cool house.

Types of Equipment

There are various types of electrical heating equipment. Those most commonly in use are:

    electric horticultural tubes
    fans
    water-filled installations heated by an electric element.

Tubular heating is the most widely used and the least expensive. The tubes – which are from 2 to 12 ft long and must be of the horticultural type – are fixed to the walls or may be stood on the floor. Their number can be easily added to at need. They have a very long life.

Fans are simple to install and may be fixed or movable. They blow warm air through the house and this movement of air seems to be agreeable to plants. In summer they can be used to circulate the air without heat, and are thus apt for a carnation or chrysanthemum house. They are probably a slight improvement on the tube, but, being made of moving parts, wear out in time.

Water-filled heaters are valuable for providing a little humidity as well as heat, thus creating good conditions for a wide range of plants. Under thermostat control they give a much more even, unvarying temperature than the others.

There are a few variations on these themes, such as plastic hot air ducts and flexible tubing. All have their uses.

How Much Heat?

Whatever kind of equipment is installed, the amount of heating required has to be calculated according to the size of the greenhouse and the nature of the plants to be grown in it and for this purpose there are useful rules-of-thumb.

First, you tot up the area of glass that there is in the walls and roof, counting the incidental wood or metal in the glazing bars, ventilators, etc., as glass. In an all-glass, dutch-light style of structure of 12 ft × 8 ft, with a height of 7 ft to the ridge of the roof and 5 ft to the eaves, this glass area will add up to 324 sq. ft.

We must now discover how much heat will be needed to cover this surface. To do so, we must start by some basic assumption of the minimum outdoor temperature and in this country as a whole it is not safe to put this higher than 20°. If our intent is to run a cool greenhouse at 45°, we have therefore to provide enough heat to raise the greenhouse temperature through 25°. This is discovered by multiplying 324 by the magic number 11, the answer being 3,564 watts. In terms of tubular heating, this means 60 ft, which, in 1965, will cost about £22.

If our 12 ft × 8 ft greenhouse is not completely of glass, but stands on brick walls 2 ft high, there will be quite a material reduction, each square foot of brick surface being reckoned as 6 sq. in. of glass. This means the equivalent of 284 sq. ft. or 3,124 watts, which means 52 ft of tubular heating.

What are going to be the costs of running this amount of heat? Here you divide the total glass area by another magic number, which is 40 for the greater part of England, the answer being in shillings per week. Thus our all-glass house of 12 ft × 8 ft will cost a shade over 45p a week and the one with brick walls a shade over 40p. A 10 ft × 6 ft lean-to will come to approximately 30p a week. These figures are appreciably lower in south-west England and appreciably higher in Scotland.*

Other Uses of Electricity

The uses of electricity in the greenhouse by no means end at heating the air in it. Gadgets can be fitted for automatic watering from either above the plants or at root level. Other gadgets will electrically fumigate it against insect pests. Automatic (non-electrical) ventilation can be fitted at tolerable cost and without running costs – one of the greatest of boons, liberating the gardener from the constant adjustment which is otherwise needed and which his daily avocation or movements often debar him from doing. Alternatively, ventilation can be done electrically by extractor fans.

Thus, apart from the actual culture of the plants, an almost completely robot greenhouse is at one's disposal, so that one can go off on holiday with an easy mind.

* The Electrical Development Association calculates on a more scientific method.

Soil Warming

Another very valuable use of electricity is to warm the soil – the soil of an outside garden frame, the soil of a propagating box (see Chapter V) or the soil of the greenhouse border. This is done by buried warming cables. Electricity thus enables the modern gardener of little experience to achieve, in the greenhouse border, or in the frame, what older gardeners did with such great skill in the manure 'hot bed' – raising vegetables and fruit to perfection much earlier than in the open and at a time when they are expensive in the shops. With only a modicum of skill one can thus raise melons, tomatoes, peaches, nectarines, grapes and many vegetables.

In the greenhouse border and in the garden frame a minimum of six watts per foot is needed but no thermostat; the current can be turned off from, say, 10 a.m. till 8 p.m. To produce real 'hot bed' conditions in the outdoor frame, the air in it also needs to be warmed. This is done by fixing air-warming cables round the inside walls of the frame; 12 watts per sq. ft is needed here, with a rod-type thermostat. The switch can be in the dwelling house, but a switch at the site is needed also.

Warning. As garden tools will be used in the greenhouse border and in the frame, safety precautions must be taken by installing a transformer to convert the mains current to a lower voltage. *Always switch off the current before doing any cultivation in the soil.* Mains cables are permissible only in beds of sand where they will remain undisturbed.

CHAPTER IV

GREENHOUSE MANAGEMENT

HYGIENE – NATURAL ENEMIES – LIGHT – VENTILATION – HUMIDITY – FEEDING

WORKING IN A greenhouse brings one into very intimate contact with plants, from which, by experience or instruction, one comes to learn their moods and their needs. We are trying to train the plant to live in artificial conditions, but, quite apart from the soil in which they are put to grow, there are some basic requirements of nature that they insist upon. These, in broad terms, are:

Hygiene;
Protection against natural enemies;
Feeding;
The right amount of light;
The right amount of ventilation;
The right amount of humidity;
The right amount of heat.

The last four, in the manner in which I have expressed them, beg the question and we have in each case to discover what is 'the right amount'.

Hygiene

The first law is cleanliness. The greenhouse is a terrible place for accumulating dirt if one is not scrupulous and after dirt comes disease. The whole place must be kept clean, especially the woodwork and the floor. Scraps of rubbish, soil droppings, decaying leaves, prunings and so on, must be cleared away promptly. Wash down the glass inside and out, at least as often as you do those of your sitting-room. Paint all wood and metal parts normally so treated before they begin to look shabby, using nothing but white paint on the inside.

Natural Enemies

These include insect pests, fungus diseases and viruses. I deal with them briefly in the last chapter. Their entry into the house is made easier by lack of hygiene, but, however careful you are, you must be prepared for their arrival, for arrive they will and some are difficult to tackle. Be prepared in advance with a good syringe, a good insecticide and a good fungicide. For insects, fumigation is an even better weapon than attack by syringe. It can be done by electrically operated aerosols or by manually lit 'smokes' that fill the whole house. Get the smoke generator or 'bomb' of the right capacity for your house, which you must be able to shut up tight, to prevent the escape of the fumes. Close all the ventilators and walk out of the house as soon as you have ignited the material. Lock the door behind you and take away the key. The fumes do no good to Man.

Light

Basically, all the plants we normally grow in a greenhouse need ample light, but some less than others. Gloxinias, orchids, ferns and many other plants require a degree of shade. From October to April maximum light should be allowed, seeing that the glass is clear; but in summer the light, and likewise the heat of the sun, will become too intense for a great many other plants and some form of shading must be provided to prevent plants from wilting.

This can be done by painting the glass with whiting, distemper or Corry's 'Summer Cloud', but these, once put on, stay on until washed off. If used, these should generally be applied in May and washed off in September. All that is needed is just enough to break the rays of the sun.

Light and shade can therefore be better controlled by fitting of blinds. There are many types. Some give dappled light and others provide heavier shading. Blinds which are fixed so that they can be pulled up and down at short notice are useful. Made in sections, one side of the greenhouse, or even sections of the same side, can be shaded separately. This is an advantage where difficult types of plants are being grown.

Several firms make sun blinds and those made by Robert Hall & Co., of Tunbridge Wells, can be recommended. They are light, strong, weather resistant, and being made of cedar wood are not liable to warp. They are easy to fix, being controlled by a cord.

Where it is not possible to fix blinds of the lathe type, tiffany or hessian can be used. While these materials cannot be pulled up and down in the same way as other blinds, they are not difficult to move.

Ventilation

Profoundly important. Ventilation goes hand-in-hand with heat control and with humidity control, but, like them, is very much a matter of experience and judgement. Broadly speaking, the first rule is to ventilate fully, especially from the ventilators in the roof. Encourage a free circulation of air without draughts. The general conception is to have everything wide open at high noon in summer and everything shut up on winter nights and between these two extremes there will be infinite variations. In summer, if the lights have been left open all day, shut them up before sundown, unless the weather is abnormally hot, and open them up first thing in the morning. When in doubt, it is better to give some ventilation than none, but in winter, frosts, draughts, dampness and fog should be kept out. When there is a strong wind, keep the lights on that side of the house shut.

This problem is very largely taken care of automatically, however, by use of the equipment mentioned in the previous chapter.

Humidity

As I have said, this is a factor closely associated with ventilation. Plants vary a great deal in their atmospheric needs, as my later chapters will show, but in general the things to avoid are very dry atmospheres and very stuffy ones. The aim should be to achieve what old hands call a 'buoyant' atmosphere – so hard to explain, so obvious to the senses.

Here again, however, we can supply some general guiding principles. The colder the weather the less the watering. Water plants only sufficiently to keep them from flagging and turn on the heat when the air becomes raw and moisture-laden. In summer, on the contrary, water the plants well, syringe the foliage, sprinkle the floor, the staging and the soil borders beneath it daily or twice daily as needed. Look over all plants to see that they are not drying out. The standard test for this is to give each pot a tap with the knuckles or with a reel of cotton fixed on the end of a stick; if the pot rings hollow, water is needed.

Beware, however, of over-watering. A too humid atmosphere invites red spider and thrips, two of the worst enemies of the greenhouse.

Feeding

Apart from the ingredients present in the potting compost, no feeding is necessary immediately after potting off or potting on, or at any time until the roots are well established.

Do not apply fertilizers while the plants are dormant, or the soil is dry, or the temperature is very low. When increased growth is required, give a feed rich in nitrogen. To encourage flower-bud formation as well as the development of tubers and bulbs, larger quantities of potash and phosphate are needed.

For plants in normal growth, the widely advertised liquid fertilizers can be depended upon. These include Liquinure,

Maxicrop, and powder fertilizers such as Clay's and Florina, the last two usually being applied dry and watered in thoroughly.

In the long run, organic manures and fertilizers bring best results, although alternate dressing of organic and inorganic liquid manures can be given. Maxicrop is made from seaweed and so is organic.

Liquid manure can be homemade by placing a bag of manure and soot in water. After stirring and diluting it, use when it is the colour of weak tea.

CHAPTER V

PROPAGATION

PLANTS CAN BE raised by:

Seed;
Cuttings and Layers;
Division and offsets.

Plenty of plants can be raised by these means without any heat at all. Indeed, there are some annuals in particular that must be seeded in the places in the open ground where they are intended to stay. We shall not be concerned with such, but with plants that can be started by one or other of these means under glass and then transplanted into their permanent quarters. Our interest will be in plants whose permanent quarters will be the greenhouse, but the gardener can, of course, use his greenhouse and his frame for raising plants that he will afterwards put outdoors.

The Propagating Box

A valuable, though not essential apparatus for raising from seed or cuttings is the heated propagating box. For the hardier plants that are to go outdoors, it can be used with as good effect in the cold house as in the heated one. It is in itself a miniature heated greenhouse. In the ordinary glasshouse it is the air space which is warmed; in a propagator we heat the soil. Whereas a close, stuffy atmosphere should be avoided in the greenhouse, quite frequently this is just what is needed in a propagator. This is to encourage the quick germination of seed or the quick rooting of cuttings.

Old-time gardeners used to plunge their seed boxes over the hot water pipes, giving what is generally known as 'bottom heat'. This corresponds to what is now referred to as 'soil warming'. Since in many houses there are now no water pipes, bottom heat is supplied by electric bulbs, by soil warming cables and even by small oil lamps.

Quite satisfactory propagating boxes can be made by the 'Do-it-yourself' man. The elementary needs are a deep box (say of 12 in.) which has no gaps in it whatever, a close-

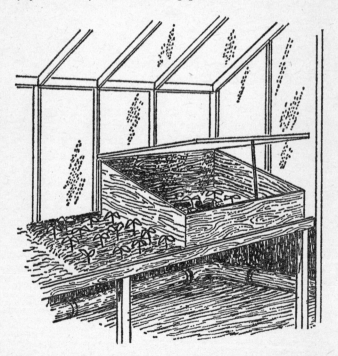

FIG. 2. Showing a bed on the staging for starting cuttings and a propagating frame

fitting glass or polythene top and an electric bulb, which may be of only 25 watts, if electric current is available, and if you know how to ensure safety.

The most satisfactory, however, are propagating boxes in which the heat is applied to the soil, by the same means as the heated frame or greenhouse border. These also you can make yourself or there are numerous models on the market.

A loading of $7\frac{1}{2}$ watts per ft is needed. The cables may be of mains voltage if one likes, as they will not be disturbed by gardening implements. They are snaked over a bed of damp sand about 2 in. deep and a further 2 in. is spread on top. The pans, pots or boxes of seed or cuttings are laid on the sand and are packed round with peat. Both sand and peat must be damp.

A soil thermostat is necessary but there need be no air heating inside the box if the greenhouse is heated, unless the plants are tropicals needing 65° to 70°.

Mist Propagation

This is the most up-to-date method of raising plants from cuttings. Many that could formerly be raised only by the skilled cultivator now present no difficulty.

The heart of this ingenious device is a very small absorbent pad, often called an 'artificial leaf'. When the pad, like the foliage of the cuttings, dries out under atmospheric conditions, a magnetic valve opens to release a very fine mist. As soon as a film of moisture from this mist has formed over the pad the valve closes. So it goes on, day and night, automatically. A fascinating toy and a wonderful boon to gardeners with difficult or large numbers of plants to raise.

Composts

Frequent mention will be found in these pages of John Innes Composts. These are soil mixture formulae devised by the John Innes Horticultural Institute for seed-sowing and for various stages of potting. They are not proprietary articles and anyone can make them who has the means. They are now widely sold in shops and many of them are pretty bogus. Go, therefore, to a really reliable supplier. They must be used within a month of having been mixed.

The formulae will be found in the appendices together with a guide to the quantities needed.

The J.I. Composts, however, are by no means essential. For anything not very precious you can make your own composts, especially if you have a small stack of rotting turves that have been sandwiched with a little manure. This provides excellent fibrous loam, which can be rubbed through a sieve, to be mixed with the requisite quantities of 'sharp' horticultural sand (not soft builder's sand) and a good grade of horticultural peat. These are the bases of all composts.

Seed

Seed can be sown in shallow boxes, in pots or in clay pans. First, cover all drainage holes or slits with crocks (see Appendix). In pots, add to them a few decaying oak or beech leaves or some nubbly pieces of soil. Then fill up the receptacle with J.I. Seed Compost to a little short of the brim – sufficient to allow watering. In default of the J.I. Compost, make one yourself of the one part each (by bulk, not weight) of sifted loam, sharp sand, and granulated peat.

The compost must be thoroughly damp; if it is not, water it well and let the water drain away. Take precautions against the 'damping-off' disease (see last Chapter).

Press down the soil fairly firmly with a pressing board, so that it is level and tolerably compact. Sow the seed, sparsely, and cover with a sifting of fine soil. Very small seed needs a mere dusting over.

Cover the receptacle with a sheet of glass and then a sheet of brown paper. Remove the paper as soon as germination starts, raise the glass half-an-inch with very short pegs until all seedlings are well through and put the boxes, etc., on a shelf close up under the glass of the greenhouse, to prevent the seedlings from becoming drawn and 'leggy'; unless they are begonias, gloxinias, or others that need a close, humid atmosphere, which should be kept on the staging.

The first leaves to appear (usually a pair) are the 'seed

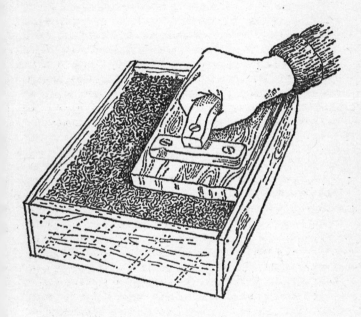

FIG. 3. Preparing a seed tray. Note the easily made wooden pressing board

leaves' which were already formed in the seed. The 'true' leaves do not appear until a little later. When they do the seedlings can be lifted and pricked-out (see Appendix) into other receptacles at wider spacing.

To do this, loosen the soil a little with a small implement, such as a 'widger' or the point of a wooden label, take hold of the seedling gently by its leaves (not stem) and, with a little leverage from below with the implement, lift out the seedling with a little ball of soil adhering to its roots.

Transplant it into the new receptacle by making a hole in the soil a little larger than the root area of the seedling, drop in the seedling to about the same depth as it was growing before and firm it all round with your fingers. Water gently with a fine rose on the can.

These new receptacles may be the permanent homes of the plants, but more often they will be but intermediate ones in which they will grow on until they are 2 or 3 in. high, according to their kind.

They are then, if intended for the greenhouse, ready for their first potting. This is usually into small pots of the 60 or 48 size (see Appendix), using the J.I. Potting Compost No. 1, or a home-made mixture of two parts loam, one each of peat and coarse sand. Always crock well, plant firmly and water with a fine rose.

Most plants will need to go into larger pots as soon as their roots begin to fill the first one. For this, you may need J.I. No. 2 or No. 3 Potting Compost, as given for each sort from Chapter VI onwards, No. 3 being needed for chrysanthemums, tomatoes, and a few other plants. A home-made substitute for No. 3 could be as before, but some added nourishment can now be mixed in, such as a little old, decayed manure, or the 'J.I. Base' which is a blend of fertilizers.

Pot firmly, using the potting stick mentioned in an earlier chapter. Press firmly all round the edges of the pot, but do not ram so firmly that the soil becomes compacted.

Cuttings

A cutting is some part of a plant, usually a side-shoot from a main stem, which, when inserted in the ground, develops into a new plant identical to its parent. There are also root cuttings, as in phloxes, and leaf cuttings, as in some begonias. Stem cuttings may be of either 'hard' wood, as in many shrubs, or 'soft' wood, as in some other shrubs and as in border plants.

Stem cuttings may be either 'nodal' or 'heel'. A nodal cutting is one which is cut *immediately* below a node, which is the slightly plump spot from which leaves emerge. It must be made with a clean and very sharp knife, an old razor blade being excellent for softer subjects.

A heel cutting is a side stem taken by plucking it off at the point where it joins a main stem by a sharpish downward twist, taking a fragment of the main stem with it, the soft skin of which is trimmed off.

Stem cuttings, whether heel or nodal, should be from firm, short-joined shoots of the current season's growth which have not flowered. The length depends on the kind of plant; cuttings of pelargoniums ('geraniums'), chrysanthemums and dahlias would be 2 to 3 in. long. Put the cuttings in a jar of water as soon as you have taken them.

The compost can be home-made, a suitable one for most things being equal parts of fibrous loam, coarse sand and peat; the sand is very important for cuttings and very often cuttings are rooted in sand alone. Another new medium that many people favour is vermiculite.

Trim off the lower leaves of the cutting, leaving perhaps four at the top (more are acceptable for carnations). Make a small hole in the pot or pan with a pointed stick or pencil, insert the cutting and press firmly all round it, making sure that the base of the cutting is in firm, intimate contact with the soil.

Cuttings, unlike seed, are best planted as close together as possible. A rooting 'hormone' such as Seradix, may be used to encourage a good start, but is not necessary with the easier things such as hydrangeas and carnations.

Subsequent treatment of the cuttings is to keep them in a close, humid atmosphere. This means a propagating box of some sort or a frame. In default, a great many cuttings are quite happy in a pot covered by a polythene bag which is held in position above the cuttings by stiff wire or short canes and held to the pot by elastic bands.

Provided this close atmosphere is supplied, plenty of plant cuttings need no heat if taken in summer, such as hydrangeas, fuchsias, ericas and pinks.

The time for taking cuttings varies greatly. Dahlias, chrysanthemums, and carnations are taken early in the year, pelargoniums at the end of August; but most greenhouse material is taken in June or July, when the new growth begins to harden.

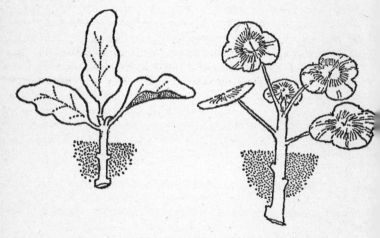

FIG. 4. Nodal cuttings of Viola and Zonal Pelargonium

As soon as the cuttings have rooted well, knock them out of the pot, pot up each plant separately and keep it in the shade for a few days.

Leaf Cuttings

Begonias and some other plants, of a succulent nature, can be propagated from leaf cuttings. For this purpose make up a box or pan of sandy soil and, having detached a suitable leaf, push the stalk into the compost at an angle of 45°. This is a good method with African violets and streptocarpus and particularly the Rex begonias. In the case of fleshy leaved plants, including begonias, selected leaves can be laid on the surface of a moist compost, fixing them down with bent wire or even hairpins. If the midrib is almost severed in several places, this will encourage a rooting system to develop and eventually each rooted portion can be potted.

Division

This simply means dividing the crown of a plant into several pieces, each with some roots, and replanting them separately. It is a common method in the herbaceous border, but not much practised in the greenhouse. Breaking up clumps of bulbs, as in daffodils, is also a form of division.

CHAPTER VI

FLOWERING PERENNIALS

IT IS IMPOSSIBLE in my small compass to describe all the flowering plants which can be grown in a small greenhouse. I must therefore select those which are easy to cultivate and which, for at least a year or two, will not take up too much room.

Many can be raised from seed, the others being obtainable in plant form from nurserymen specializing in greenhouse plants. All mentioned are of fairly easy culture and respond well to any extra attention given.

African Violets, See *Saintpaulia*

Anigozanthus coccinea, sometimes known as Kangaroo's Paw, is an attractive cool greenhouse perennial plant, which has been grown in this country for nearly 150 years. The plant itself grows about a foot high, the woolly, reddish flower stems being up to 2 ft and carrying bright green flowers. These are split on one side towards the tip, which reflexes to expose the yellow anthers, the appearance of which suggests the claws of an animal. The inner surface of the flower is a greyish-green colour.

The variety *manglesii* is particularly attractive, growing $2\frac{1}{2}$ to 3 ft high, the showy green and red flowers appearing in July.

The plant is raised from seed sown evenly and thinly in seed boxes or pans of moist light sandy loam, to which a little sifted decayed manure has been added. A suitable temperature is 50° to 55°. Once the seedlings can be handled they should be pricked off and later moved to 3 in. pots.

Sometimes a sooty substance appears at the tip of the leaves, particularly on the older ones. This can be trimmed off or the plants sprayed with a fungicide.

Established plants can be divided in the spring, and potted in the usual way, when they will flower during the summer.

Azaleas. The beautiful little flowering shrubs that adorn our houses in winter are known in the florists' trade by the non-valid name of 'Azalea indica', or Indian azaleas, though they do not come from India. They are varieties of a rhododendron species and few plants can rival them for showiness. Most of the plants used for forcing come from Belgium, arriving during September and October.

They vary in size, but most will be suitable for planting in 48-size pots, although the bigger specimens should go into 32s and the small plants into large 60s.

In most cases the root ball will have to be reduced in size before potting is done, and it may be necessary to chop off a fairly thick portion to enable the azalea to go into a pot of a suitable size for the amount of top growth.

The potting mixture should be lime-free and consist of fine soil, peat, and leaf-mould. It should be rammed well down the side of the pots, otherwise, when watering is done, the moisture will run through the pot without soaking the root ball, thus causing the plant to wilt and lose its leaves.

After potting, plunge the pots into water to the level of the soil in them, then stand them for a week or two in a cool house or frame to recover, before forcing begins, but they will need full ventilation.

Gradually increase the temperature so that it can be held at night around 50° with a consistently moist atmosphere. When fresh growth is seen raise the heat, so that it is never less than 65°. Water must be applied with care for although it would be fatal to allow the roots to dry out, the new fibrous roots of forced azaleas are quite fine, and will quickly suffer if they become waterlogged.

Overhead sprayings of water can be given until the time the flower buds begin to break. Keep the atmosphere moist. In addition to being right for the azaleas, this will discourage attacks from thrips or red spider, the only likely pests which can gain a hold under dry conditions.

Named varieties of *Azalea indica* which have proved good are: Petrick alba, white; Princess Beatrix, deep salmon-pink; Mme Petrick, deep pink; and Mme Yan, an attractive light salmon-pink.

Although indica varieties are the most widely grown of azaleas for winter flowering, there are several other types which can be brought into the greenhouse. They may not flower quite so early, but they are attractive for pot work. These include the varieties often recommended for growing in the front of the border or rock garden. They are generally referred to as 'dwarf evergreen azaleas'. The following respond to the same treatment as recommended for Azalea indica: Yodogawa, lavender; macrantha, deep salmon; Hinomayo, bright pink; Hinodegiri, carmine, and obtusa latifolia, crimson.

Busy Lizzie. See *Impatiens*.

Calceolarias. Often known as Slipper Flowers. Another old name for these plants is Cats' Boxing Gloves. They are bushy little plants, with pouch-like flowers in yellow, brown, or red, often freckled. It is the herbaceous species and varieties that are so useful for the small greenhouse.

Sow in July, using the John Innes or similar compost. Press this firmly, then apply a dusting of fine silver sand before sowing very thinly. Moisten the compost by holding the pan in water; never apply water from above. Growth will be seen in seven to ten days. The weakest looking seedlings often produce the best blooms.

When the second leaf forms, prick out the seedlings placing them $1\frac{1}{2}$ in. apart, so that they have room to develop. Keep in a shaded frame for four weeks or so, then move to $2\frac{1}{2}$-in. pots, and later to a bigger size.

House the plants at the end of September, standing them on a base of gravel or coarse ashes, which are kept moist to ensure the compost does not dry out. In winter, keep them in a temperature of not less than 45°. Support as necessary.

Once the flower buds become enlarged, overhead spraying should stop, a drier atmosphere being necessary, although fairly frequent sprayings of water between the pots will help to maintain cool conditions.

Varieties: Albert Kent hybrids, 15 in.; multiflora nana hybrids, 9 in., and the new multiflora F.1. hybrids. A shrubby species is *C. integrifolia,* also known as *C. rugosa.*

It takes eight or nine months from the time the seed is sown for full flowering plants to be produced.

Canna. Tall, subtropical plants bearing large, flaglike flowers in various colours. They grow from a rhizome, which is a thick, fleshy stem-base.

Start the rhizomes into growth from February onwards, in a temperature of about 60° to 70°. They can be potted up singly, or started in moist peat or leaf-mould on the green-house staging. There, they can be packed closely together. When growth is evident, potting should not be delayed, for the roots quickly lengthen and become entangled and break easily.

While the average rhizome will fit into a 5-in. pot, some specimens may need a larger size. Large rhizomes can be carefully cut in two, so long as each portion has a good strong growing bud. It is usual to divide the rhizomes for propagating purposes. Seed can be used but is often slow and uneven in germinating. Sow from January to April, in a temperature of not less than 70°.

Seedlings are potted as growth proceeds, until they reach the 5- to 6-in. pot size. Extra decayed manure at the bottom of the larger pots will help growth.

Towards the end of April they should be transferred to the cold house. Attention must be given to watering, and ventilation given during the daytime.

A selection of named varieties is available in shades of pink and red, as well as orange and white. The old Roi Humbert, with rich orange-scarlet flowers and shining dark bronze foliage, remains a firm favourite.

Christmas Rose. See *Helleborus.*

CINERARIAS. Among the most colourful of all pot plants, cinerarias, with their large, brilliant daisy-form flowers, are easily raised from seed sown in succession from May until August. Earliest sowings provide colour from December onwards and by sowing a pinch of seed at intervals of twenty-one days, batches of flowering plants will be available until April.

Germination is usually quick and regular. When the seedlings can be handled, move them to thumb size pots, and give shade until well established. As growth develops move to larger size pots using the John Innes Compost No. 2, or a simple mixture of three parts loam, and one part each of silver sand, leaf-mould and old manure is most suitable, especially if a sprinkling of wood ash can be added.

To encourage sturdy growth, keep the pots in a well ventilated frame and shade from strong sunlight. The seedlings will need watering almost daily. *Do not let moisture settle on the crown.* The compost should be porous enough to allow water to seep through. At the end of September move the plants to the greenhouse, keeping them in a temperature around 50°.

The majority will be quite happy in 5-in. pots, but vigorous specimens can be given a bigger size. High temperatures cause thin, spindly growth. Overhead sprayings of clear water will improve the condition of the plants.

When the flower stems show, feeds of liquid manure at seven- to ten-day intervals will encourage good development although they must stop once the flowers begin to open. Always pot firmly, but do not bury the crowns.

Cinerarias are inclined to be rather dirty plants unless looked after properly, green fly being a particular menace. Derris will normally clear this pest, although if the trouble is particularly persistent and occurs on other plants too, the use of an Azobenzene smoke cone will probably be more efficient. These cones should not be used when the flowers are open or while the foliage is moist. Look out for leaf miner also (see last Chapter).

The best strains for general purposes are *Cineraria grandiflora*, with large daisy-like flowers, and *C. stellata*, with star-like blooms. Particularly useful for the small greenhouse is Teicher's Jubilee Mixed, which is early flowering, of dwarf, neat habit, having small foliage in a handsome colour range.

An interesting new strain, producing more than 60 per cent of double or semi-double flowers of crested and pin-cushion forms, is Gubler's Double Mixed. The colours in this mixture include pinks, crimson and blue. Since the flowers are double, they last considerably longer than the normal single types.

Columnea is closely related to the *saintpaulia*, which gives an indication of its requirements. Freedom from draughts and full light, but not strong sunshine are needed, a north or east aspect being ideal.

Columneas are excellent for hanging baskets, where their trailing growths are a delight. A suitable rooting medium consists of leaf-mould, peat and silver sand, used in hanging baskets lined with sphagnum moss. Avoid over-watering, although sufficient moisture must always be available. Once the flower buds begin to open, in June, give occasional feeds of liquid manure. Cuttings 2 or 3 in. long can be taken in spring, rooting them in a sandy compost in a warm atmosphere.

There are many species including banksii, gloriosa, kewensis and schiedena, all with orange or orange-scarlet flowers which spring from the axils of the leaf stems, which grow 15 to 18 in. long.

Erica. The pot ericas or Cape Heaths are good winter and spring greenhouse plants. The best species for the small greenhouse is *Erica gracilis*. This flowers from October to February and is therefore excellent as a Christmas pot plant. It has reddish-pink flowers, and has a number of forms bearing blooms of pink, red, white or lilac. *Erica hyemalis* is also excellent, having red or white flowers from October onwards.

Propagation is by seeds or cuttings. Cuttings can be taken

from August to February; the earliest ones being rooted without artificial heat. Secure them by detaching more or less mature side shoots with a heel, which should be made smooth before inserting them in pots or boxes of loam, peat and silver sand. Shade them from bright sunlight. After a couple of months, the rooted cuttings will be ready for potting.

Overhead sprayings are beneficial. Once the flower buds begin to develop, liquid feeds will be helpful. During summer move the plants to a cold frame or sheltered place outdoors.

Seed can be sown in the spring, the seedlings being potted up in the usual way.

Euphorbia pulcherrima. Better known as the poinsettia, this is one of the most showy of winter plants. The flowers are insignificant; it is the scarlet bracts which are so showy. These form large flattish heads of vivid colour often measuring up to 15 in. across.

It is best to propagate young plants each year from cuttings although old plants may be grown for several years, provided they are pruned hard in the spring. To secure cuttings, cut back selected plants to about half their length, keeping them in a dry, frost proof greenhouse.

Towards the end of April, the plants should be started into growth by giving them a soaking of water and moving them to a temperature of 55° to 60°. If syringed regularly, they will soon produce side growths which, when 3 or 4 in. long, can be taken and inserted as cuttings.

Cuttings of this plant are apt to bleed freely and should therefore be dipped in powdered charcoal. For rooting, use small pots filled with sandy compost and, having dipped the end of the cuttings in the powdered charcoal, insert them in the compost and stand the pots in the cold frame without delay, or keep them in a cooler part of the greenhouse. Then the plants will not flag or wilt much and should soon form roots.

It is not usually wise to move plants from small to large pots but this can be done with poinsettias, since they dislike root disturbance. Once the plants are 5 or 6 in. high they should be grown under cool conditions and may be placed out of doors in a sheltered position during July and August.

FUCHSIA. This is a most popular summer flowering plant. Good ventilation and atmospheric moisture are keys to success. A temperature of 50° is ideal, excepting during the resting period, when it can be as low as 35° to 40°. Fuchsias object to direct sunlight, so that some shading is necessary to prevent severe checks.

Repotting needs to be done from time to time, for, although it is a mistake to provide pots which are too large, it is equally wrong to keep the roots so restricted that they become matted into a hard ball. When potting, make sure that the pots are clean and dry. This makes it easier when the next move is required. After providing crocks for drainage material, place a thin layer of leaf-mould or peat over these before putting in the soil, which should be worked in around and between the roots.

Although fuchsias can be raised from seed, germination is often erratic and prolonged and one cannot be sure that anything worthwhile will be secured. The best method of propagation is to take cuttings of young shoots. These normally root very easily throughout the spring and summer, especially if they are placed in a sandy compost and kept in close, moist conditions for a time.

Once it is evident that the cuttings have rooted, they can be moved to lower temperatures and potted up singly. A moist, cool atmosphere helps the plants to make even growth. Pinch out the growing point to encourage bushy habit. Side shoots also can be stopped to keep the plants compact. Once the plants are growing well, liquid fertilizer can be applied. It can be given at fourteen-day intervals until the plants are actually in flower.

With sufficient root room and good soil, they can be kept for some years. They should be rested in winter in a frost-proof place. Very little water is then necessary. When starting the plants into growth in February, give the soil a good soaking. Prune out all badly placed, weak shoots.

The fuchsia is adaptable and can be trained into fan and other shapes as well as standards. Good rich soil should be regarded as essential for best results.

For the greenhouse, there are countless varieties, both double and single flowered. Among the best are:

> Abbé Farges, semi-double, cerise and lilac.
> Achievement, reddish-cerise and rosy-purple.
> Ballet Girl, double, crimson and white.
> Blue Gown, cerise and violet-blue.
> Cascade, carmine and white, trailing habit.
> Fascination, red and rose-pink.
> Lena, flesh-coloured sepals, purple corolla.
> Marinka, crimson-scarlet shaded rose.
> Rose of Castille, blush-pink and violet-purple.
> Swanley Yellow, orange-pink and vermilion.
> Thalia, long orange-scarlet flowers, bronze foliage.

There are also several excellent varieties with ornamental foliage, including Sunray, of which the leaf edges are marked cream and cerise.

Geranium. See *Pelargonium.*

Gerbera. The Barberton Daisy, *G. jamesonii*, from South Africa, with elegant, long-petalled orange-scarlet flowers on 18-in. stems from June to October, has given rise to some even more elegant hybrids. These take in a colour range of terra-cotta, apricot and amber.

Propagation is by seed or division. For 100 per cent germination it is essential for seed to be fresh. This is not always easy since the majority of seed is imported.

Sow in trays or pots of well drained compost. Stand the seed upright rather than sowing it flat in the usual way. For quick growth give fairly heavy shading with a regular temperature of about 70°. After germination, remove the shading but do not subject the seedlings to direct sunshine.

Never bury the crown or heart of the plant. A surface

application of some dry material, such as coarse sand or shingle, between the plants will keep them in good condition if the crown is just above the mulch.

From twenty-eight to thirty-two days will elapse between bud development and the opening of the flowers. Gerberas are not specially susceptible to pest attacks. Green fly, white fly and leaf miner, are possibilities and can be controlled by spraying.

Helleborous Niger. The Christmas Rose is a hardy subject, but the pure white petals are liable to be spoiled by frosts and cold winds when the plants are grown outdoors.

When planted in the ordinary warm greenhouse flowers can be available from December until February. *Helleborus niger praecox,* produces flowers a little smaller than those of the main variety. This drawback is offset by the fact that it can easily be forced under glass. The form known as *maximus* also forces well. All have pure white flowers.

Stock should be secured in March and April, and placed 12 to 15 in. apart in beds in the open, planting a little on the deep side. A good fibrous loam to which leaf-mould has been added is suitable, especially if a dressing of old farm yard manure can be worked in. This will help in retaining moisture during dry weather.

Lift the plants in early October, making sure to keep a ball of soil around the roots. Once the plants are in the greenhouse, keep them in darkness or otherwise shaded for a time, to encourage the stems to grow to a length of 10 to 12 in.

A temperature of around 55° is about right and this should remain even, with atmospheric humidity. Once the flower stems have reached the required length, the buds will be clearly seen, and the shading material can then be removed. Tests have proved that, normally, the flowers will be ready for cutting about a week after the plants are in full light.

Hydrangea. There are well over thirty species of hydrangeas, including the climbing forms. The kind grown as pot plants for the greenhouse decoration consists of varieties of the species *H. macrophylla*. These are first class for the cool greenhouse where they can be had in flower over a long period. If wanted for flowering in March, the plants must be brought into warmth at the end of December.

The finest flower heads are obtained when the plants are started off at 60° and where the atmosphere is fairly humid. After a week or ten days, the temperature should be increased to 65°. Keep them well watered when in full growth and regularly supply weak liquid manure in February. Gradually lower the temperature to about 60°.

Properly grown plants, raised from summer cuttings, should produce plants with anything from fifteen to twenty flower heads, while from spring cuttings five to seven flower heads will be produced.

Blue flowers are obtained by adding aluminium sulphate to the potting compost at the rate of about 1 lb. per barrow load of soil. Do this in July, when potting for the last time. Use fortnightly a solution of aluminium and iron sulphate at the rate of 1 oz. to a gallon of water.

Varieties for forcing: Mme Emile Mouilliere, white. Ami Pasquier and President Goumer, red. Holstein Hamburg and Altona (good for blueing) pink. My Darling, deep pink, (can be blued) and Europa, pink (very suitable for blueing).

For later forcing, La France and Louis Sauvage are two good pink varieties which are excellent for forcing and blueing.

Impatiens. *I. holstii* is a first class pot plant of quick, vigorous growth, producing its red flowers over a long period. The *I. holstii* hybrids take in a good colour range, including salmon-pink, and orange-scarlet. All grow 18 to 24 in. high, although there is a dwarf named sort with vermilion-red flowers.

Impatiens sultani is an attractive and easy species from Zanzibar. A perennial, it has achieved wider notice than the other balsams because of its common name of 'Busy Lizzie', a name given, presumably, because the plant produces its rose-scarlet flowers with such continuity. It should have a winter temperature of 58° to 65°. Growing 1 and 2 ft high it looks well in 5-in. pots. Old plants can be trimmed into shape in February and given fresh pots and soil. Cuttings from strong side shoots can be taken from March to August and started in pots of sandy soil. They root best in a closed frame. Plants can be raised from seed sown in the spring in a temperature of 60°.

I. sultani nana, is dwarfer. For those who like really dwarf balsams there are the new Orange Baby and Scarlet Baby. Both grow about 4 in. high and flower most freely.

Kalanchoe. Natives of South Africa, kalanchoes are half-hardy succulent plants, with thick, roundish serrated leaves and clusters of attractive flowers in red, pink, yellow or orange-yellow. Most of the improved new sorts grow 18 to 20 in. high.

Among the best-known sorts are *K. carnea*, pink; *K. flammea*, orange-scarlet; and *K. lanceolara*, having flowers in shades of orange and salmon-yellow. Probably the best known of all varieties, however, is *K. blossfeldiana*, a bright flaming red. This was named after Robert Blossfield, a successful German grower, who did much to improve the kalanchoes.

Cuttings 2 in. long, may be taken from August until February, but obviously those taken in winter will take longer to produce flowering plants than those rooted earlier. They can be rooted in a mixture of sandy-loam and peat, although some gardeners use equal parts of silver sand and peat.

Plants can be raised from seed, in the same way as recommended for begonias, gloxinias and saintpaulias. A temperature of 70° results in quick germination. Once good growth has been made the temperature should be 10° lower.

PELARGONIUM. In popular speech, pelargoniums are commonly called 'geraniums', a name that properly belongs to a quite different, hardy plant for the outdoor border or shrubland. No pelargoniums are hardy. There are several classes.

Regal or Show Pelargoniums. These superb green-house plants have single or double flowers which are usually striped or blotched, the plush petals often being crinkled. The colour range is wide, from almost black through violet and magenta, to the most showy orange, and going on to very pale pink and white. They need just a little more care than the commoner zonal pelargoniums of public parks and

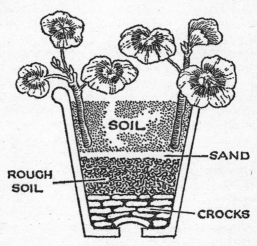

FIG. 5. Zonal Pelargonium cuttings inserted round the edge of a flower pot

bedding schemes, but are by no means difficult. Showy plants can be had in flower during spring or early summer.

They are propagated from cuttings of firm young growth, which can be taken from May to early August. These should be about 3 in. long, and a clean cut should be made at the base, immediately below a leaf joint. Remove the lower leaves and bracts before inserting in pots or trays of sandy compost. The compost should consist of one part loam, two parts peat and three parts silver sand.

If sand is sprinkled on the top of the compost some will fall into the holes when the cuttings are dibbled in. This will help to improve drainage, aerate the compost and encourage good growth. Move to bigger pots according to growth.

When the plants come into flower, feed with liquid manure at ten-day intervals, making sure the roots never become dry. After flowering, cut them back fairly hard, to prevent their becoming leggy. From June to September they can be placed outdoors in a frame or other sheltered place. This hardens the wood in readiness for the future season's flowering.

Varieties: Apple Blossom, rose-pink, on white ground. Black Velvet, black upper petals edged purple. Caprice, deep rose-red. Carisbrooke, huge rose-pink, deep maroon blotch, one of the finest. Carnival, cerise-red.

Countess of Feversham, soft carmine-rose, flared maroon. Diadem, velvety lavender and deep purple. Grand Slam, large rosy-red flowers, upper petals violet red, very fine indeed. King Midas, orange red shading to apricot. Lady Irene Burton, orange-pink with bold maroon blotch, flowers lightly held against the deep green foliage.

Lord Bute or Purple Robe, perhaps the most striking of this section, small exquisitely edged flowers, deepest velvety purple with intense carmine edge. Muriel Harris, pure white, amethyst pencilling.

Rhodomine, large rhododendron-like flowers of a delicate mauve, with white throat. San Diego, or Quakeress, orchid-mauve, bold purple splash.

Zonal Pelargoniums. These are the commoner 'geraniums', much used for bedding out in public parks and Victorian gardens and now much in favour again. They are very easy to grow and are rarely attacked by pests or disease. With good culture they remain ornamental in foliage or flower almost all the year round. Plenty of light, good rooting conditions with moisture as required, ventilation and freedom from frosts will give them every opportunity to flourish.

Cuttings should be taken in August or early September

for summer flowering, or in early spring for winter blooming. Choose plants which make short jointed growth from the base. A mixture of loam, peat and sand, encourages a sturdy root system. Once it is evident that the cuttings are growing, move them to 3-in. pots. Keep them growing through the winter, in a temperature of about 50°.

In the spring, they should be ready for moving to 5-in. pots. Pinch back young shoots occasionally, to encourage bushy growth. Given plenty of light and warmth, they should soon flower freely. Do not feed in any way until there is a good root system. A plant or two can be carefully knocked out of their pots to determine this. Fed too soon, geraniums will make a lot of leafy growth with few flowers. Keep faded flowers removed.

Established plants should be kept fairly dry at the roots during the winter to give them a partial rest. Repot or top-dress in the early spring. Zonal pelargoniums can be stood out of doors during the summer. This not only gives additional space but helps to build up sturdy growth. The same treatment is needed by both the variegated-leaved and the scented-leaved sorts. The latter can be kept for many years, although it certainly pays to take a few cuttings annually to ensure a supply of strong young plants always being available.

Zonal varieties: Red shades: Decorator, semi-double, crimson-scarlet. Elizabeth Cartwright, carmine-red, small white eye. Gustav Emich, freely produced, semi-double scarlet. Paul Crampel, reliable old scarlet variety.

Pink, salmon and rose shades: King of Denmark, deservedly popular, with large trusses of semi-double salmon-pink on sturdy, short-jointed plants. Millfield Rival, clear pink, white eye. The Speaker, semi-double salmon-pink.

White: Hermine, best double white variety. Queen of Whites, freely produced white flowers. White Magic, semi-double, pure white.

White, marked and fancy: Carmel, white, edged cherry-red. Fortune, double white, margined and flushed pink. Lady

Warwick, white with picotee edge of pink. Staplegrove Fancy, large flowers, edged and spotted pink.

Magenta, purple and crimson: A. M. Mayne, double, purple-crimson, strong grower. Belvedere Glory, magenta-pink. Festiva maxima, double purple of excellent bloom, sometimes said to be the same as A. M. Mayne, although some blooms at least lack the crimson shading, resulting in a really fine purple.

Orange and orange-scarlet: Orangesonne, outstanding, double orange flowers, very fine. Sansovino, large single orange flowers.

Ivy-leaved Pelargoniums. These can be grown either as upright specimens, being tied to light supports and grown against the greenhouse wall or pillar, or they can be allowed to trail naturally. They will withstand a good measure of rough treatment and even neglect and poor soil, and yet give a good display of colour. Besides this, when it is necessary to restrict the growth of the stems, the plants do not object to their growing points being constantly pinched out; in fact, the leaves then often assume an especially clean, glossy, dark green colour, and maintain a good shape.

It pays to take cuttings annually. The stems are thinner, harder and longer-jointed than the Zonals. Another difference is that, whereas the latter will keep on throwing flower spikes in rapid succession, the ivy-leaved sorts seem to produce a lot of blooms at one time, when the plants are literally covered with colour, and then have a short rest, afterwards producing another great profusion of flower heads.

Varieties: Abel Carrière, double orchid-purple. Alice Crousse, double magenta. Galilee, double rose-pink. La France, lilac feathered maroon, very popular. Mrs W. A. R. Clifton, orient-red, white markings. Snowdrift, double white. Sir Percy Blakeney, geranium-lake.

Variegated-Leaved Pelargoniums. These are grown for the colour of their foliage, the flowers in many cases being insignificant.

Varieties: Caroline Schmidt, white variegation. Chelsea

Gem, silver white. Crystal Palace Gem, golden, with deeper markings. Distinction, olive green, black zone. Harrison Weir, chocolate on yellow ground. Lass of Gowrie, silver tricolor. Miss Burdett Coutts, creamy-yellow variegation. Mr Henry Cox, bronze, red and yellow.

Scented-leaved Pelargoniums. These never fail to attract attention and if slightly pressed or rubbed with the fingers all emit a perfume.

Species: P. crispum 'Prince Rupert', lemon scented. *P. tomentosum*, peppermint. *P. capitatum* and *P. denticulatum*, rose scented. *P. odoratissimum*, apple scented. 'Clorinda', eucalyptus. *P. quercifolium*, pungent scented. *P. parviflorum*, coconut scented.

Poinsettia. See *Euphorbia.*

Primulas. The greenhouse primulas are easy to manage and make delightful pot plants, flowering in winter and spring. There are four species.

Primula obconica often flowers intermittently throughout the year. Seed of this species can be sown in a sandy compost from March to May, in a temperature of 60° to 65°. Prick out and pot up the seedlings in the usual way.

Germination is sometimes irregular. Plenty of crocks should be used in the pots, for drainage must be good. The colour range is very wide and apart from the mixtures, named sorts can be obtained. The leaves of this species irritate the skin of some people who should therefore grow other types.

Primula malacoides is a most dainty plant for the cool greenhouse. Its flowers are carried on whorls or tiers 9 to 12 in. high. Colours include lilac, mauve, pink, salmon, and white. Good plants have ten to twelve spikes showing colour at the same time. Sow under cool conditions in May and June.

The Chinese primula, *P. sinensis*, which includes the stellata or star-shaped forms, also takes in many colours, including shades of pinks, red, blue, and white. These should be sown in April.

Primula kewensis, which has powdery leaves, is noteworthy, since it produces yellow flowers and needs less heat than other species. Sow in June or July, using a sandy compost. For the final potting, give less peat and manure than used for other sorts. A temperature of 45° to 50° is suitable and the flowers show from early February onwards. Never bury the crowns of any primulas, otherwise they will decay.

Miniature Roses are usually grown as alpines, but they are also first-class pot plants for the greenhouse.

If you have, or can secure, good sized specimens in $3\frac{1}{2}$-in. pots, which perhaps are a little on the big side, these are ideal for propagation. Move them to 5-in. pots and then bring them into the cool greenhouse after trimming them back and removing any dead or old wood.

Suitable material for cuttings are shoots with three joints. Remove flower buds and lower leaves, and prepare in the usual way. Then insert in pots or pans of sandy loam or pure silver sand.

Put one or two cuttings in thumb sized pots or a larger number in small 60s. Eventually, move each cutting into a $2\frac{1}{2}$-in. pot, using the J.I. No. 2 Compost. Keep the plants in a cold frame until they are established.

Another method of propagating miniature roses is by sowing seeds under glass in a temperature of 60°, fairly early in the year.

Seed is usually offered as 'Rosa nana multiflora' or 'Fairy Roses'. Seedlings will vary in height from 6 to 12 in., while the flowers produced will be single, semi-double or double, in shades of pink and red.

There are many named varieties, which must be propagated from cuttings. These include:

Bo-Peep, 6 in., pink; Maid Marion, 9 in., velvety scarlet; Polly Flinders, 7 in., copper-orange; Simple Simon, 6 in., deep pink; Tinker Bell, 10 in., rosy-red; and Baby Masquerade, one of the best, with yellow buds opening to salmon, flame and red.

SAINTPAULIA. Better known as African Violets, these

delightful plants were first discovered in East Africa in 1890. In its native place, the Saintpaulia grows in various situations in woods, forests and between rocks. It does best in fairly rich, damp soil and succeeds in a wide temperature range, but never below 40°.

Saintpaulias need light and, particularly in winter, as much sunshine as possible. During summer, however, they can be improved by providing slight shading. Abundant dark green foliage with no flowers is a sign of too little light. Very pale leaves, with short stalks, indicates too much sunshine.

To keep saintpaulias in good condition, they should be in a temperature of between 60° and 70°, although this will probably drop 10° at night. Extremes in temperature are a cause of non-flowering. Free ventilation without draughts should be provided.

Water as necessary and use that which has the chill off. Very cold water causes leaf spotting. It is best to stand the pots in saucers of water so that moisture seeps up through the compost, but do not leave the pots in water. When top watering, do not make the crown of the plant wet. Liquid fertilizer at fourteen-day intervals will be of great help.

African violet leaves sometimes become dusty. It is quite a good plan to blow off the dust with light bellows, but the best way is to wash the leaves. To do this, hold the pot in the hand in a fashion to keep the soil and plant in position. Then gently move in slightly warm water. This job must be done very carefully since the leaves are brittle and liable to snap off if moved sharply. After the wash, stand the plants in a warm position out of draughts and sun, until the leaves dry off.

Perhaps the most important thing observed with the African violet is the great importance of a *humid atmosphere*. In a mixed house, this is not always easy. The simplest way, however, is to stand the pots in trays of sand damped with hot water, when the steam will provide the necessary humidity. In periods of dry weather spray the leaves with clear water.

Propagation of saintpaulias can be carried out by sowing seeds, taking leaf cuttings, or by dividing the plants. Seeds should be sown on the surface of a fine soil mixture. In a temperature of 65° to 70° seedlings will be seen within twelve to fifteen days. Prick them out early to avoid damping off. Lever them out with a thin stick and transfer to a peaty compost. Later, move to small pots and then to the larger sizes as growth develops.

Leaf cuttings should be taken off with an inch of stem. This and the lower part of the leaf should be inserted in pans of silver sand in the warm. Roots form quickly at the bottom of the leaf. When fresh young leaves appear, pot the little plants separately. Sometimes it is possible to detach off-shoots from established plants and pot them up separately.

Salvia. *Salvia splendens*, the scarlet sage, is a tender perennial from Brazil, much used for bedding-out schemes and suitable also for the greenhouse. Seed is often slow and erratic in germinating. Sow in January and February for the earliest flowering plants. If a temperature around 65° cannot be maintained, defer sowing until March. Prick off the seedlings into boxes, later moving them to 3-in. pots, giving larger sizes as growth proceeds. For bedding-out in the open garden, transplant in the last days of May.

Varieties: St John's Fire, 12 in., bright red. Blaze of Fire, vivid scarlet, 12–16 in. Scarlet Pigmy, 6 in. Harbinger and New Dwarf Scarlet, 15–18 in.

Other colours not so strident as the scarlet-flowered sorts include: alba, white; carnea, flesh-pink; rosea, rose-pink; violacea, violet; Pink Rouge, salmon-rose and Violet Crown, violet-purple, all growing 12 in.

Salvia patens is a beautiful Cambridge blue, some 18 in. high, but not so free flowering as the scarlet varieties. Of Mexican origin, it is a tender perennial, although easily flowered as a half-hardy annual.

Sow early in the year, in a temperature of 60° to 65°. Prick out and pot up in the usual way and, since this species forms tubers, provide pots large enough to allow these to develop, unless it is intended to transplant them outdoors in the first week of June.

Tubers of *S. patens* can be stored in winter and started again the following season.

Strelitzias. *Strelitzia reginae* is a unique and striking plant. It has the common name of Bird of Paradise Flower from the resemblance of its large flower to the head of a bird. It will thrive in any cool glasshouse. The aim should be to maintain a minimum winter temperature of 50°.

This plant owes its name to Queen Charlotte of Mecklenburg-Strelitz, wife of George III. The flowers are produced on stout stems $2\frac{1}{2}$ to 3 ft high, sometimes more, which stand out well from the foliage. Starting to bloom in early summer, they remain in full beauty for a long period.

Normally repotting is done in the spring, although it can be done at other times as necessary, but not in winter.

Pot firmly, using a mixture of three parts sandy loam, and one part each of peat and well decayed manure. Water moderately until new growth is seen, after which plenty will be needed until the autumn. During hot weather, frequent syringings will be helpful. These will freshen the plants, and keep down red spider, while occasional fumigation will deal with thrips.

To propagate, detach suckers in the spring, and pot up. Keep them in a warm moist house until well rooted. Seed is sometimes available, although germination is irregular. A fairly humid atmosphere with a temperature of 65° to 75° is advisable. It takes about four years to secure flowering plants from seed.

Trachelium caeruleum is a half-hardy perennial for the cool or cold greenhouse, having the common name of Blue Throatwort. During July and August, the large dense heads of small, lavender-blue, fluffy blossoms brighten the rather solid looking plants.

Oakworth glasshouse

Hartley brick-based metal house

Small Crittall metal house

Pratten house, showing side and top ventilator

Messenger Sun Loggia

Strawson house with chain lath blinds, keeping out up to 10° of frost

Crittall metal lean-to

Small electric propagator

Introduced from Southern Europe in 1640, this plant belongs to the campanula family and grows 2 to 3 ft high. The best specimens are obtained by sowing in July or August. Pots, pans, or boxes should be used and after sowing in the John Innes or similar seed compost, keep the receptacles shaded until germination takes place.

Pot the seedlings singly when they can be handled. If the main growths are pinched out occasionally, really bushy, free flowering growths will develop.

The plants may be placed in the cold frame until October, and then moved to larger sized pots, a little well rotted manure being added to the final compost. Keep them on the dry side during the winter, but give plenty of water during spring and summer.

Once the flower heads begin to show, weak liquid manure may be given at seven-day intervals. Although the plants will flower year after year, it is best to raise a new stock annually. Apart from seed sowing, cuttings of young shoots may be secured and rooted in April or September. There is a white form, but this is not nearly so decorative.

Streptocarpus. This is best known as the Cape Primrose, a summer and autumn flowering perennial plant remarkable for the abundance of large tubular blooms produced well above the foliage.

It belongs to the same family as the begonia and gloxinia and needs similar treatment to these subjects. They all like a peaty soil. Seed should be sown early in the year in a temperature of 60 deg. F., and the young plants potted on until they reach the five or six-inch size pot. When in full growth feed with liquid manure. Keep them on the dry side during winter. S. wendlandii has violet and white flowers, while S. dunii is rose, although a mixed strain will give a wide colour range.

CHAPTER VII

ANNUALS FOR SPRING COLOUR

MANY OF THE gay annual flowers, both hardy and half-hardy, normally grown in the open garden make handsome decorations for the greenhouse with the minimum of heat or for the enclosed porch attached to the dwelling-house. Not everyone who sees the magnificent displays of flowers from seed at Chelsea and other spring flower shows, realizes that many of them have been grown in comparatively cool greenhouse conditions throughout the winter.

It is partly the result of their having had a long growing season that the plants are so sturdy and free flowering. Unhurried growth leads to bushy, well balanced plants.

A greenhouse where a winter temperature of 45° can be maintained is quite adequate. Sowing should be done in August. The greenhouse will then become a place full of promise throughout the winter, leading to a lovely display during the days of spring and early summer. Here are a few suggestions.

The dwarf cornflowers Jubilee Gem and Rose Lady, both make excellent pot plants and, for something white, I have had success with the ordinary candytuft, of which the seeds can be sown individually.

Clarkia and godetia are no trouble, although I find it best to sow very thinly so that the roots do not become tangled. Mixtures of these look showy but separate colours can be grown if preferred. If something fairly tall is needed, try larkspurs. The double stock-flowered sorts grow 2½ to 3 ft high, while the Giant Imperial varieties, pink or dark blue, will sometimes reach 4 ft, branching well from the base.

You should certainly try the annual delphinium Blue Butterfly, growing 15 in. high with brilliant deep blue flowers; it is one of the most charming plants for the green-house. Echium or Viper's Bugloss deserves consideration, making compact plants a foot high, which become smothered in flowers. The mixed hybrids take in a charming colour range, chiefly in shades of pink, lilac, purple and blue.

The dwarf French marigolds make nice rounded plants and, apart from the mixtures, Spry (9 in.), yellow and mahogany, and the Marionette varieties (6 in.), in shades of gold and chestnut-crimson, are specially good.

Calendula, the familiar English or pot marigold, is excellent for sowing in August. Adaptable and foolproof, the plants produce a plentiful supply of long-lasting flowers. Apart from the 'double art shades', Orange King, Goldfink, and Radar are most reliable. The seedlings transplant easily with little check.

I have had great success from August and September sowings of nemesia and Phlox drummondii, growing three or four plants in a 5-in. pot. They are best wintered in boxes and potted off in early March. Then they will commence flowering very early in May.

Salpiglossis are particularly useful where taller plants are required. The prettily-veined trumpets are in rich shades of purple, pink and red. A few little twiggy sticks placed in the pots will keep growth upright.

Mignonette, too, is easy to manage and will flower from late March onwards. For further variety you can try *Alonsoa warscewiczii*, orange-scarlet (15 in.) or Brachycome Blue Gem, the Swan River Daisy, which is excellent in pots (9 in.). All transplant well.

There is another annual which I recommend for sowing in August. This is something altogether larger. It is *Lavatera trimestris*, the best varieties of which, in a large pot, will easily grow 4 or 5 ft high, and, well grown, maybe 3 ft in diameter. One plant in a 7- or 8-in. pot looks lovely, but three plants in the 10-in. size provide a superb decoration. Sow in seed pans or pots of a fine, porous compost, placing them in a lightly shaded frame or under cloches. As soon as possible move the seedlings to 3-in. pots, using a coarser compost. These should be returned to the frame, keeping them as near the glass as possible.

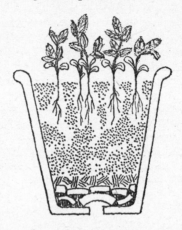

FIG. 6. Seedlings pricked off into a 5-inch pot

By the third week in October, the young plants should be ready for 6-in. pots, which should be kept in the greenhouse near the glass, to encourage short jointed growth. They will then grow steadily and can be moved to their final pots in February. Use six parts fibrous loam and one part each of coarse silver sand and decayed manure. A sprinkling of crushed charcoal and mortar rubble or lime, are useful additions. Once the flower buds show, liquid manure can be given at ten-day intervals. Of the varieties of *Lavatera trimestris* available, Pink Domino and Loveliness are specially good, the latter being a really fine deep pink sort. A white flowered form is also obtainable.

Firm potting and a central supporting cane are needed, for the lateral shoots will require tying in as they develop. Remove the growing points when the side shoots are about 18 in. high.

Viscaria is easily grown, the modern dwarf growing types being so much better than the older strains which were of straggly habit and never looked nice. The sweet scented nicotiana or tobacco plant, with white or pink flowers, can be grown in the shaded part of the greenhouse, the flowers being especially fragrant in the evening.

Schizanthus, the Butterfly Flower or Poor Man's Orchid, is a greenhouse annual *par excellence*. The freely produced flowers on bushy plants are in shades of pink, crimson, mauve and white, many being prettily marked. Get a packet of mixed colours and sow in August or September, and again in January if you like. Keep them close up to the light when young and pot them on as necessary into 5-in. pots. Pinch out the tips after first potting to encourage bushy growth. A cool house temperature of 45° is quite enough. Ventilate freely.

CHAPTER VIII

BULBS, CORMS AND TUBERS

THERE ARE MANY bulbs, corms and tubers which are first class for pots and bowls as well as the border. It is essential to start all of them under cool conditions, so that roots form before there is much top growth. All should have regular supplies of moisture during their growing period.

Achimenes. Gay, easy and long-lasting flowers, very popular for hanging baskets, but good for pots also. The tubers are available in mixture from January until April. Use a fine mixture of loam, peat, sand and well decayed manure. Bury the tubers an inch deep. Once top growth appears plenty of light and regular watering are needed. The tubular flowers appear on 15- to 18-in. stems which need light support unless grown in hanging baskets.

Antholyza aethiopica has showy, 3-ft spikes of tubular red and yellow flowers, rather like montbretias in appearance. Plant 3 in. deep in early spring. Seed can be sown in boxes of sandy loam, in gentle heat. *A. crocosmoides* has spikes of brilliant red and golden-yellow blooms in September.

Arum lilies. An invalid name for the handsome plants previously called callas and richardias, but now officially named zantedeschias. These plants have for many years been much in demand for decoration purposes, particularly at Eastertime. They are not lilies.

Tubers can be potted towards the end of July for flowering from December onwards. August plantings provide bloom from February to late April, which includes the Easter period.

Although arums can be grown in the greenhouse border, there is the drawback that the plants must remain in position for almost twelve months. Where space is limited, pots are more convenient.

For border planting, use well cultivated soil, working in bone-meal at the rate of 3 oz. per sq. yd and a dusting of soot. Space the tubers 12 in. apart and leave their tops just showing.

Although overhead sprayings will be useful as growth develops, the soil must not become soggy. Look out for 'fly' which often settles on the young growths, and fumigate as necessary. A temperature of about 60° is suitable.

From early December, the plants should be given fortnightly feeds of liquid manure, applied close to the soil. Good roots produce two to four flowers.

Zantedeschia aethiopica, the white species, is the most popular; *Z. elliotiana* is yellow and later flowering.

After flowering, gradually dry off the plants and lay the pots on their sides in a sunny place until the next season.

BEGONIAS. There are both tuberous and fibrous rooted species and varieties; the former are the best known since they include the large and handsome hybrid varieties, as big as paeonies. There are many sumptuous named varieties; unnamed sorts can be bought by colour selection at less cost and give good results. These are often listed as *B. multiflora*. Pendulous varieties are fine for hanging baskets.

Use firm, plump tubers, starting them (dimpled side uppermost) in shallow boxes of about 3 in. in depth. At the bottom, place a layer of leaf-mould or peat, then cover with a good mixture made of one part each, loam, peat, or leaf-mould, and half a part of silver sand, or it is possible to use peat only. Make the mixture damp at planting time but not sticky. The custom has been to place the tubers in the soil so that the crowns are left uncovered, but Mr S. C. Langdon, of the famous firm of Blackmore and Langdon, advises that tubers should be pressed into the compost so that the crowns are covered. Cover the trays or pots with paper until the first signs of growth are seen.

A temperature of 60° to 65° is right for starting the tubers;

if lower, growth will be slow. As growth proceeds, move the plants to 5-in. pots. For vigorous growers, even larger pots can be used. Liquid feeding can be given when the flower buds begin to appear.

At the end of the growing season, gradually withhold water so that the tubers can be dried off. Keep them in a frost-proof, airy place during the winter.

Rex begonias are grown for their large, handsome, marbled leaves, much loved of flower arrangers. They should have some shade. There are now several different forms, some being of upright branching habit, often growing very large. Others are spiral-leaved and there is a group of miniature Rex varieties.

Begonia 'Iron Cross' was brought from the East Indies by Mr Maurice Mason of King's Lynn. The dark markings on the green leaves are very prominent. Somewhat smaller is *B. versicolor*, of Chinese origin. Of the Asian sorts, *B. bowerii* and *B. hereaceifolia* are well known. *B. langeana* has heart-shaped leaves; 'Silver Star' is a splendid American hybrid.

Rhizomatous sorts prefer to be shielded from the sun. They like warmth and humidity, but not damp conditions. Propagation is by stem and leaf cuttings, while some can be raised from seed.

Begonia semperflorens is a fibrous-rooted species, very dwarf, with multitudinous single flowers, much used for outdoor bedding, but quite suitable for pot work.

Clivias are of easy culture, with attractive, freely produced umbels of funnel-shaped flowers on sturdy stems. They flourish in the cool greenhouse. The best known is *C. miniata*. It has bright green, strap-shaped leaves, growing from 18 to 24 in. long, and the 15- to 18-in. stem is surmounted with an umbel of twelve to eighteen companulate, scarlet flowers, having a yellow throat.

C. nobilis is smaller than *miniata*, and has orange-red flowers, the petals being tipped with green. *C. gardenii* has orange-red petals green tipped. The flowers of all varieties

Begonia masoniana

Begonia socotrana 'Mrs Leopold de Rothschild'

Calceolaria x multiflora 'Nana'

Chrysanthemum 'John Rowe Supreme'

Cineraria multiflora

Cyclamen persicum 'Giganteum'

Cymbidium Babylon 'Castle Hill'

Epiphyllum ackermannii

are scented and usually followed by large, attractive, brilliant red berries.

Seed can be sown in spring, but this is a long process. It is easier to propagate by removing the fleshy off-shoots in February or March. A compost of two parts loam, one part decayed manure plus silver sand and a dusting of charcoal, suits the plants which like plenty of moisture during their growing period. The roots should only be disturbed when it is necessary to divide them, in fact, clivias seem to flower better when pot bound. Established plants will benefit from occasional applications of organic liquid manure.

CYCLAMEN PERSICUM has few equals for winter and early spring display. The best time to sow seed is during August and September; this will provide plants for flowering during the winter of the following year. It is also possible to sow seed in the early part of the year, with the object of securing flowers from December onwards, but results are not so good by this method.

Use pans or trays of fairly rich compost and space the quite large seeds $\frac{1}{2}$ in. apart. Cover them with up to $\frac{1}{4}$ in. of compost and after placing the pans in a temperature of 60° to 70° cover with paper to prevent the surface soil drying out. As soon as the seedlings have produced leaves, move them singly to small pots. Rich compost is not needed and a mixture of 2 parts loam, 1 part of leaf-mould and a half part of silver sand is suitable.

Keep the seedlings in the light, but out of direct sunshine and preferably where there is a moist atmosphere. By early April, the young plants will be ready for moving to 3-in. pots. In early July they will be ready for well drained 5-in. pots, in which they will flower. For this final move, add some decayed manure or bone-meal to the compost. Do not bury the corms too deeply but leave the top exposed.

In July, stand the plants on a hard base in the cold frame, shade from sunlight and make sure the roots do not dry out.

In September move the plants to the greenhouse again, standing them on the staging in full light. When the flower buds appear, give liquid manure at seven- to ten-day intervals until the flowers begin to open. Avoid draughts, although fresh air is helpful. Any leaf or flower stems which show signs of damping-off should be removed. After flowering, gradually withhold water and remove the plants to the cold frame again. There they can rest until August, when they can be repotted for flowering the following winter. Cyclamen can be grown for two or three years with perfectly good results and there are cases where they have gone on giving a show for many years.

Apart from the Grandiflora hybrids there are several other strains of seed including: Papilio Mixed, with prettily frilled petals; Sweet Scented mixed; and the new Sakata double mixed, which are F.1 hybrids.

Corms, of course, can be purchased through bulb merchants.

Freesias are graceful and fragrant giving them a high decorative value. Use a good compost consisting of 3 parts fibrous loam, and 1 part each of peat and silver sand, plus a sprinkling of bone-meal is very suitable. Alternatively, the John Innes Compost No. 2 can be used. Plant in August or September.

Six or seven corms are placed $1\frac{1}{2}$ in. deep in 5-in. pots, which should have a layer of crocks over the bottom, to ensure good drainage. After planting, stand in a cold frame or outdoors in a sheltered position, on a bed of cinders or stones, but the pots should not be covered, as is usually done with other bulbs. Water should be given sparingly until top growth develops.

Before frosts come, the pots should be taken into the cool greenhouse, stood close to the light and a few twigs inserted near the young foliage to keep it from falling over. Any extra growths appearing in the pot must be removed in order to direct the strength of the plant to the main flowering stems. When the flower spikes are seen, apply weak liquid manure at ten-day intervals. Too much heat in the early stages is a cause of blindness. A temperature of 50° is sufficient.

Nowadays varieties can be had in many colours, but the sweetest scents are to be found in the old, white *Freesia refracta alba* and in the cream and yellow varieties. Flowering normally begins early in February and goes on to the spring months.

Gladiolus. The popular, large-flowered outdoor hybrids can be very easily grown in the greenhouse at minimum heat if desired and will give early bloom. There is better greenhouse value, however, in the less hardy varieties of *G. colvillei* and *nanus*, which are dainty and altogether charming.

In November plant four or five corms in a 5- or 6-in. pot. Kept cool, they flower in April.

Varieties: Blushing Bride, ivory-white; Amanda Mahy, salmon-pink; The Bride, pure white; Peach Blossom, delicate rose, and Spitfire, brilliant red with crimson blotch. All are beautiful.

Gloxinias. This lovely summer-flowering plant produces large, velvety trumpets in shades of red, pink, lilac and white. It can be treated in the same way as tuberous begonias. Warm, moist conditions with shade from direct sunshine, and light, peaty soil are needed for success.

Seed can be sown early in the year, in a temperature of about 65° and, with good treatment, the plants will flower within six months of sowing. The dust-like seed should be sown thinly in a sandy compost. The seedlings will be seen within a fortnight and must be pricked out early, subsequently being moved to pots. Keep the little tubers slightly above the soil level to prevent damping off.

Particularly good plants can be propagated from leaf cuttings. For this, use medium sized leaves with a piece of leaf stalk attached and insert in peaty soil in a propagating box. Tubers will soon form and can be grown in the usual way.

Gloxinia tubers are available from specialist firms and should be started in March. As the flower buds begin to swell, give liquid manure at ten-day intervals. After the flowering period, gradually dry off the tubers and store them during the winter in a dry, frost proof place.

Hippeastrum. These gorgeously coloured bulbous plants used to be known as Amaryllis. They produce in spring and early summer large lily-form trumpets in many colours, and have long strap-shaped leaves. If forced, they can be had in bloom from early February onwards.

The bulbs should be placed singly in well drained 5- or 6-in. pots, covering them up only to two-thirds of their depth with rich sandy compost. Growth will soon begin and the flower spike develops very quickly, the leaves following much more slowly and not attaining their full length until the flower spike is beginning to pass over.

Plenty of moisture is needed until the leaves show signs of withering. Keep the plants in a temperature of around 60°. As the leaves begin to die down, reduce watering progressively until, by autumn, the soil is nearly dry.

Repotting is only necessary every three or four years. Each spring remove an inch or so of top soil and replace it with a rich compost.

Although there are several species of hippeastrum, the bulbs are usually offered simply in separate colours.

Hyacinths are most accommodating and, excepting for the forcing varieties for Christmas flowering, can be grown without any heat at all. The Roman and Prepared varieties should be potted in August, the tops of the bulbs being left exposed, and plunged outdoors under leaf-mould or weathered ashes for five or six weeks.

After taking the plants out of the plunge, gradually introduce them to the light, otherwise growth will be checked and the leaves become discoloured. Do not give much water until the bulbs are well rooted. There are many varieties to choose from in the catalogues of bulb merchants.

Hymenocallis (or **Ismene**), popularly known as the Peruvian daffodil, is a sweetly scented, very decorative, white flower with a large trumpet backed by long, narrow, curling, ribbon-like members, which are the perianth of the flower. It is of easy culture. Pot the bulbs from February onwards, using sandy, turfy loam, well decayed manure, or coarse silver sand. As growth proceeds, the pots should be watered freely. Keep in a temperature of not less than 65° during the summer. Repot once in three years.

Hymenocallis calathina and its improved form, 'Advance', grows about 2 ft, is white, striped green at the throat and is the species usually grown. Others are:

H. 'Sulphur Queen', creamy-yellow trumpet; *H. macleana*, narrow leaves, white funnel-shaped flowers, striped green. *H. speciosa*, also known as Pancratium, has scented white flowers. *H. macrostephena*, white, greenish shading.

Ixias, or 'Corn Lilies', have graceful, wiry, strong stems 15 to 18 in. high, producing six or more flowers of most striking beauty. All have a prominent dark centre and make ideal cut flowers. Give exactly the same culture as for freesias, but the pots are best plunged up to their rims in ashes, and left in a sheltered position until February. If brought into the cool house they will soon produce a fine show of blooms. Ixias are best increased by offsets or seed can be sown in heat in the spring.

LILIES. There are many lilies which respond to pot treatment and they are certainly not difficult to grow. It is a mistake to use large pots or tubs. A large pot of soil which is constantly watered will quickly go sour if it is not more or less filled with roots.

Some varieties are stem-rooting and must be planted so that room is left for top-dressing with rich compost when the bulbs are in growth.

Good drainage should be provided. This will prevent loss of soil through the hole and, equally important, stop the outlet from becoming clogged and causing sourness.

The exact soil mixture to use will largely depend on the lilies being grown, some species liking, even preferring, an abundance of leaf-mould, others, which must have sharp drainage, needing additional silver sand. Fibrous loam is the chief ingredient in all mixtures. Other items can be added or used in varying quantities according to specific preference.

A simple mixture would consist of three parts good fibrous loam (and the fibrous content is important), 1 part each of coarse silver sand and leaf-mould, the latter preferably being fine and coming from beech or oak leaves. To each bushel of these three mixed together, add 2 oz. of bonemeal or hoof-and-horn, or, if available, 1 part of *old* sifted manure (cow or stable).

With the exception of a very few species, notably *L. candidum* and *L. testaceum*, which need to be covered with only an inch of compost, non-stem-rooting lilies should be up to 3 in. below the surface, depending on the size of the bulb.

Stem-rooting kinds should have their tops about 4 in. below the pot or tub rim. Once the stem roots are visible, they need to be covered. Successive coverings are usually necessary, according to the way which the stem roots are produced. Use a rich mixture such as 1 part good loam, and 2 parts decayed manure or 'ripe' compost.

If planting can be done in the autumn it should never be postponed until the spring, by which time the new roots will be developing and can easily be injured.

Lilies in pots must always be started under cool conditions.

When danger of severe weather is over, the pots should be moved into the open, but sheltered from rain and strong winds. Subsequently they can be transferred to the greenhouse.

When planting lilies, carefully spread out the roots, working the soil among them and making sure it is well firmed. When moving them to a bigger pot, remove the old drainage material, but be careful not to disturb the basal roots.

It is possible to force lilies into flower, and it is not at all unusual to get them into bloom by Easter, when they are greatly valued for church decoration. The job needs care and, to achieve the finest results, only the best, plump bulbs should be used. If bulbs are being used from the garden, mark likely specimens early in the season, and make sure the flower stem of that year has not been allowed to seed. The production of seed is strength-taking and bulbs for forcing should be absolutely vigorous and not have lost any vitality in producing seed.

The following are amongst the best lilies for greenhouse culture:

Lilium auratum, the splendid gold-rayed lily of Japan, with large white gold veined flowers dotted red. 4–5 ft.

L. chalcedonicum. Scarlet flowers with reflexed petals. 3 ft.

L. croceum. Orange, spotted black. 2 ft.

L. elegans (*maculatum*). Varieties in shades of red, orange, yellow. 2–3 ft.

L. hansonii. Yellow, spotted black. 3–4 ft.

L. japonicum (*krameri*). Pink, spotted red. 2–3 ft.

L. philippenense. Pure white, excellent for cold house. 2–3 ft.

L. regale. White, flushed rose-pink. Stem rooting. 4 ft.

L. speciosum and its colour varieties. White, spotted and marked pink. Stem rooting. 3–4 ft.

L. willmottiae. Orange-scarlet, reflexed petals. 4–5 ft.

Some lilies can be raised from seed without difficulty.

Narcissus, which includes the well-known trumpet daffodils, are easy and useful for greenhouse display. While a little heat gives earlier flowers, almost all grow quite satisfactorily in the cold house. The bulbs should be potted in August using a good fairly rich compost, or bulb fibre if bowls are employed. Cultivation as for hyacinths.

Schizostylis is often known as the Kaffir Lily. Potted in March, they produce excellent gladiolus-like flowering plants from October onwards. Do not allow them to dry out and give fertilizer from August onwards. Propagate by dividing the rhizomes in the spring. *S. coccinea* is crimson, and 'Mrs Hegarty' pink.

Sparaxis is the South African Harlequin flower, which requires exactly the same treatment as the ixia and the freesia. They grow 6–12 in. high, and have graceful, bell-shaped flowers. They have gorgeous contrasting colours and are usually sold in mixture, but the variety Scarlet Gem freely produces brilliant velvety-scarlet flowers, the black centres being prominently marked yellow. The dead flowers should be removed before they form seed pods and, if the pots are placed in a position where the corms can ripen slowly and water is gradually decreased after flowering, the same corms can be used to provide colour the following season.

Streptanthera is closely allied to the sparaxis, being of similar habit and growth. A very pleasing effect can be provided by planting five bulbs in a pot, and plunging them in the cold frame in peat or weathered ashes, bringing them indoors when an inch of growth is seen. The species *S. cuprea coccinea* has salver-shaped scarlet flowers with a dark centre, on 9-in. stems, during late May and early June.

Tigridia. This interesting and very easy plant has beautiful spotted and marked flowers, and is sometimes known as the Tiger Flower.

The irregularly shaped bulbs should be planted 2 or 3 in. deep in early spring. Use a well drained soil, consisting of loam, sand and leaf-mould. Propagation is by offsets.

From July until September tigridias provide a really unusual and striking display of colour. While the individual blooms only last a day, as soon as one passes, another is there to take its place.

All grow 18 in. high and have exotic looking flowers with quaint unusual markings and spots, a good mixture providing a truly gorgeous display.

Tulips. Of these, there are so many sections and varieties that it is possible to arrange for colour from Christmas until May. They can be grown cold or brought on in a little heat. The earliest varieties can be potted in late September, plunged outdoors and thereafter treated in the same way as hyacinths.

Vallota (Scarborough lily). *V. purpurea* is a very easy bulb, needing little or no heat and bearing scarlet trumpets. Pot the bulbs in March, one in a 5-in. pot. Water very spar-

Aladdin paraffin stove with pipes

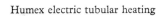

Humex electric tubular heating

Taking a cutting of a
greenhouse carnation

Potting on a young carnation

Primula malacoides

Streptocarpus, Sutton's
Triumph strain

Salpiglossis

Primula sinensis

Hybrid Gloxinia

Greenhouse Cineraria

*Campanula
isophylla mayi*

Pleione formosana,
an easy orchid

ingly until growth appears, then gradually more freely. Stop watering soon after flowering, keeping the soil barely moist from November to March.

Veltheimia is another native of South Africa, having spikes of small, pendant, densely packed tubes. The bulbs should be potted in August or September in a compost of good loam, peat, or leaf-mould, and silver sand; with the addition of well rotted manure or bonemeal. Start them in a fairly low temperature and when there are signs of growth increase the heat slightly. Flower spikes appear from the end of October until the spring. Once flowering is finished, and the leaves show signs of withering, water must be gradually withheld. From the end of April the pots can be placed in a cold frame or sheltered place to ripen. Bring them into the greenhouse again in August. Propagation is easy by offsets.

Veltheimia glauca has grey-green wavy leaves and red and yellow spotted flowers on stems about a foot high. *V. viridi-flora* is the best-known species, producing rosettes of strap-shaped wavy leaves 9 or 10 in. long and flower stems a foot or more high, bearing many reddish-yellow spotted flowers in summer.

CHAPTER IX

FOLIAGE PLANTS

HOWEVER SMALL THE greenhouse, room should be found for a few ferns and other foliage plants. There is a wide range of easily grown attractive subjects although I have room to mention only a few of the best. Several have become popular 'house plants'.

Adiantums or Maidenhair ferns. A temperature of 50° is suitable, with a moist atmosphere during the growing season. Use a compost of fibrous peat, leaf-mould and turfy loam, with some silver sand and a few pieces of charcoal. Repot in spring, when the fronds begin to uncurl. Top dress with fresh compost in March and feed with liquid manure weekly from May until August.

Propagation is by division in spring, or spores can be sown in the same way as seeds. Place them thinly on the surface of pans of finely sifted compost. Cover with glass and give light shading, setting the pots in saucers of water. At first, green moss-like growth appears, followed by the green, heart-shaped growths called prothalli. Set these in finely sifted compost and keep shaded and moist.

Adiantum cuneatum comes from Brazil and has several forms including gracilis and elegantissium.

Aralia. These plants are an example of nomenclature confusion. *A. sieboldii*, now *Fatsia japonica*, is most widely grown, being an evergreen shrubby plant. Its variety *moserii*, has larger leaves and is more compact.

Several plants in a large receptacle give a good effect and avoid the bareness of the base of the stems. Propagation from cuttings is the best method, and the only one for the variegated forms. Stem cuttings root easily in spring, and should be potted up in peaty soil and well rotted manure. Give plenty of water and liquid feeding during the summer.

Asparagus. The vegetable asparagus has some valuable foliage relatives. *A. plumosus* and *plumosus nanus* are easily raised from seed, which will usually germinate within three or four weeks of sowing, if the pots or boxes are placed in a temperature of 65°, preferably with bottom heat. March to May is the main sowing period. Move seedlings into 3-in. pots, discarding those of slow and irregular growth. Move to bigger pots as growth develops, using a simple compost such as the John Innes No. 1.

Asparagus sprengeri is treated in much the same way, although it is not quite so popular as *A. plumosus*. The roots should never lack moisture, otherwise the smaller leaflets will fall. Keep the plants out of continued sunshine and give them plenty of water.

Asplenium fern. This has fresh shiny, long fronds, and likes light and warmth.

COLEUS.

One of the finest of all foliage plants, the coleus rivals the brightest of flowers in the brilliance of its variegated foliage, in which crimson, purple, brown, white and other tints mingle. Sow seed from January onwards in a temperature of 65°, using a fine, sandy compost. Since it is so fine, it should barely be covered.

Use trays or pans of fine porous compost and sow very thinly, simply pressing the seed into the soil and applying the merest sprinkling of silver sand. Cover with glass and paper, and keep in a temperature of 60° to 65°. The paper covering gives shading and it should not be necessary to water the compost until germination occurs.

Coleus seedlings are liable to damp-off, so apply water with care. When big enough to handle, move the seedlings to other boxes or pots using the J.I. Compost No. 2 or make up a mixture of 3 parts loam, 2 parts leaf-mould and 1 part of silver sand, with some decayed manure.

When pricking out remember the smallest, weakest looking seedlings often develop into the best coloured plants. Coarse, rapid growing plants, are often those in which green is most prominent. After potting, stand the plants in a light position close to the glass. Shade from direct sunlight and give a few applications of liquid manure.

If the growing point is taken out, it encourages the production of side shoots. Well marked plants can be propagated from cuttings, but since there are now several splendid strains of seed, of which the Rainbow Master Blends is one of the

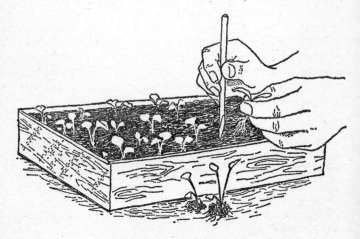

FIG. 7. Pricking out seedlings

best, it is simplest to raise a fresh batch of plants annually. Never give coleus too much root room. If kept slightly potbound, the colours become more intense.

Coleus thyrsoides is grown for its deep blue flowers in midwinter. It needs a temperature of around 65° and is propagated from cuttings in the spring.

Cordyline and **Dracaena.** These two genera of foliage plants are very similar in appearance, and at various times have been confused, and cordylines have been referred to as dracaena. There are differences, which, however, are of interest to the botanist rather than the gardener.

Cordyline may be distinguished by its creeping root stock. Although in some cases flowers are produced, they are insignificant and the chief method of propagation is by rhizome cuttings, which are planted in moist peat in a propagating case, where they soon root and can be potted up. In a moist atmosphere, aerial roots form on the stems, which can be cut into pieces and potted up separately. *C. australis* has dark green leaves, but there are several forms having either a red or yellow central strip to the leaves.

Cyperus alternifolius is easy to grow. It has erect, dark green stems of ribbon-like foliage, radiating from the top of a foot-high stem, so earning it the name of Umbrella plant. From June onwards, insignificant russet-red flowers appear in the leaf axils. The variety *gracilis* has wiry stems and narrower leaves than the type. *C. a. variegatus* is mottled and striped white.

Seeds can be sown in pans of sandy soil in a temperature of 65°. When the seedlings can be handled, pot them off singly. The roots can be divided in spring. Plenty of water and good light are all this plant needs. During summer stand the pots in saucers of water. Dry roots cause the tips of the leaves to discolour.

Cyrtomium falcatum is a hard-wearing fern that produces dark green, cut-edged, shiny leaves up to 2 ft in length. It will last for years so long as it never lacks moisture and is kept from scorching sun. Useful as a room plant.

Davallia bullata is much used in hanging baskets. It sheds its leaves annually and in the past has been largely imported from Japan.

Dracaena godseffiana is a fine, broad-leaved plant, of rather spreading habit, the dark green foliage being well dotted with bright cream spots. It likes warm conditions.

The dark-green-leaved *D. deremesis*, and *D. hookeriana*, with its variegated forms, are easy to grow and propagate.

The latter is tough and stands quite poor conditions, including draughts, and gas.

Sponge the foliage to keep it clean, but do so fairly early in the day. Do not let moisture settle at the points where the leaves join the stem.

Fittonia. These semi-creeping plants have attractive foliage and are suitable for the greenhouse and living-room. *F. verschaffeltia* is dwarf growing with dark green, beautifully netted, leaves and red veins. *F. argyroneura*, of similar habit, has bright green leaves netted with white veins.

Layering forms a ready means of propagation. The stock plants are plunged in peat in heat, and the shoots which then develop can be layered. Alternatively, cuttings are taken during the spring and summer and rooted in sand and peat, bottom heat being a help. When well rooted, move the layers or cuttings to 3½-in. pots of J.I. No. 3 Compost. Moisture and shade are needed in summer, and a watch must be kept for aphis.

Grevillea robusta is a very decorative foliage plant which is inexpensive to grow, for it comes rapidly from seed. This should be sown singly in small pots in February, using the J.I. or a similar mixture, preferably in a temperature of 65°, which can be lowered when growth is advancing. Shade from strong sunlight and ample moisture is needed. The plants look well in 5-in. pots.

Hedera. This is the botanical name of the **ivy**. They can be used as climbers or trailers, and stand up to a remarkable amount of neglect and bad treatment. They are not particular about light, in fact, the green varieties will grow in dull corners.

Almost all of the modern pot ivies are derived from *Hedera helix*, our 'common ivy', and among the best and most reliable varieties are Pittsburg, Chicago, Hahn's Self Branching, cristata, Glore de Marengo (*Canariensis variegata*), New Silver and minima, the latter having really small leaves.

Propagation is by stem cuttings which root well through the year, although summer cuttings develop more quickly.

Rooting can also be obtained by standing cuttings in water. Keep a look out for aphis. If seen, spray with a good insecticide.

Helxine soleirolii is often known as Mind Your Own Business. It will grow in any soil but should be kept out of the sunlight. It will grow over the edge of the pot when it looks quite pretty. Water from the bottom and avoid wetting the foliage. In the open garden is a choking weed.

Peperomia. A favourite among room plants. The ovate, fleshy leaves of *P. argyraea* (or *P. sandersii*) which grows 7 or 8 in. high, are a metallic white colour, overlaid with light green veins.

P. augustifolia has shiny fleshy leaves of yellow and green, while *P. glabellata* is small leaved, either green or variegated, and very suitable for room culture. *P. pulchella*, with heart-shaped leaves, and *P. incana*, with velvety foliage, are both good plants.

Most peperomias will stand a fair amount of shade, especially the green leaved kind. The others like more light.

Leaf and stem cuttings, divisions and seed are all suitable means of propagation. Take cuttings in spring, using a sandy mixture and providing a temperature of 65°. Pot on as necessary, giving liquid manure occasionally. Stop the plants to permit bushy growth, and keep them from over-dry conditions and direct sunshine. Avoid over-watering at all times. Usually grown for their ornamental leaves, some varieties produce rat's-tail-like flowers.

Phyllitis scolopendrium is the Hart's Tongue Fern, with dark green crinkly fronds. It will grow in the garden as well as in the house and is easily propagated by division.

Platycerium bifurcatum is the Stag's Horn fern, so called because of the appearance of the fronds. It prefers to be grown in peat and leaf-mould only. Never allow water to settle on the leaves.

Pteris cretica. The popular Brake fern has many forms, all with shiny, dark green, well divided, feathery fronds. It likes generous feeding and is first class for shop and general indoor decoration. It will stand dark, poor conditions as well as more congenial circumstances.

Sansevieria. This is a favourite among foliage subjects, known in the vernacular as Mother-in-law's Tongue, from their tough, narrow, thick, sword-shaped leaves. The species is *S. trifasciata* with green leaves, but the variegated varieties are most in demand. They are tolerant of neglect, but dislike wet root conditions during the winter. Propagate from suckers or offsets.

Selaginella is also of simple culture. It has moss- or fern-like foliage and can be readily propagated by cuttings. It is an ideal subject for including in groups of plants and worth growing where a moist atmosphere and shade can be maintained.

CHAPTER X

CHRYSANTHEMUMS

THE CHRYSANTHEMUM IS something of a specialist's plant, with a jargon all its own. I have space to deal with it only in a general way, for readers who are not concerned with exhibiting.

There are many hardy, perennial types as well as some annual species and varieties. It is, however, the greenhouse sorts that are the most showy. The type you can grow will depend upon the heating arrangements available.

There are different methods of culture, but the best plants are those grown in pots. These do not suffer any check, which occurs when plants are lifted from the ground and potted. A forcing temperature is not needed and if you can provide 45° from the end of February until early April, when the plants are moved to frames, this will be most suitable.

For propagation the usual procedure is to take cuttings from the end of February, according to variety, and insert them in boxes or trays of sandy soil. When they are rooted, move them singly to 3-in. pots, using a good fairly rich compost. Alternatively one, two, or three cuttings can be put in each pot, according to the freedom with which the particular variety is likely to 'break' and the number of times it will be possible to 'stop' the plants. Cuttings of the same size and vigour should be placed in the same pot.

Keep the pots in a cool temperature of 45° until the rooted cuttings are established, when they can be moved to cold frames from the beginning of April onwards. After a move to the 4½- or 5-in. pots, the plants are placed in the 8- to 10-in. size according to growth made. When risk of frosts is past, they are stood outdoors without cover but in a place where they are not likely to be damaged or blown over by winds.

Always pot firmly. Finger pressure on the compost down the sides of the larger pots, followed by two or three sharp taps with the bottom of the pot on the bench, usually works the soil in well. A blunt ended piece of wood should also be used as a rammer to work in the new soil around the sides of the pot. The soil should always be finished off 2 or 3 in. from the top of the pot, to allow for watering and top-dressing as the season advances. At each move the ball of soil should be about $\frac{1}{2}$ in. below the surface of the new soil. Light overhead sprinklings of water are helpful, especially in warm weather.

When the pots are placed outdoors from May onwards, see that they have a firm base, such as a cinder bed. Alternatively use black 150 gauge polythene sheeting, spreading this, either over entire standing grounds or in strips where the pots are to be placed. This prevents weeds from coming through. A thin layer of gravel over the polythene allows surplus water to escape or be soaked up.

Give separate cane support to each plant, which should be tied to the cane as growth develops. Water as required giving a thorough soaking and not frequent sprinklings. Begin to feed when the pots are full of roots. This can be discovered by carefully knocking out a plant to see how big its root system is.

Some 'stopping' will be needed, although the date is not important unless one is growing plants for exhibiting on a particular date. Stopping or timing means nipping off the top of the shoot resulting in the so-called 'natural break'. When more lateral shoots develop these are known as 'first crown breaks'. The catalogues of specialist nurseries give the instructions required for each variety.

The end of May or early June is a good time for the November flowering sorts, while the December varieties can be stopped twice about the middle of April and again in mid-June. If any of the November flowering plants are particularly advanced in growth, they could be stopped first in April and then in early June. If, of course, some plants are more forward than others, it would prolong the flowering period. Unwanted side shoots must be constantly removed; tying regularly done, and a watch kept for insect pests or possible diseases.

The exact date for housing pot plants will depend on the season and locality.

Pests and Diseases. Keep a good look-out for leaf-miner, eelworm and mildew, which are dealt with in the last Chapter.

Varieties. New varieties are constantly being introduced, superseding older ones rapidly. Keen growers should join the National Chrysanthemum Society. Particularly for show work, it is essential to know something about classification.

I can only give a very brief selection of sorts but these will act as a guide, to the various sections. White: Blanche Du Poitou, American Beauty, Monument, Duke of Kent, Henry Trueman, Jessie Habgood. Yellow: Constance Baker, Golden Trueman. Pink: Agnes Ford, Mary Wallace, Edith Woolman. Bronze: Majestic. Red: James Bryant, Cossack.

Good decoratives include: Balcombe Perfection (orange-bronze); Pink Superb; Elizabeth Woolman, lilac; Davos, pure white.

Reliable 'incurved' sorts are: Annie Curry, white; Connie Mayhew, cream; Vera Woolman, yellow; Shirley, Primrose; Shirley Lady, lavender, silvery-pink reverse.

Single chrysanthemums are also attractive and these include Desert Chief, orange-amber; Mason's Bronze; Molly Godfrey, pink; Broadacre, white; Woolman's Glory, terracotta bronze. Anemone-flowered chrysanthemums are also interesting and they are available in a number of good colours including: Elspeth (mauve) and Golden Nymph.

Cascade Chrysanthemums. A novel greenhouse display can be secured by growing the cascade chrysanthemums. Introduced by Sutton & Sons in 1933, they produce many single, and often scented, blossoms which are unique from a decorative point of view, because they can be trained to create a sheet of colour. Well grown, a single plant produces a cascade of flowers up to 2 ft wide and 4 ft and more long.

Sow in February or March, using boxes or pans of

compost in an even temperature of 60°. Pot the seedlings as they develop. Seed is available in mixture, but plants of special colours can be marked and trained the following season. Cuttings can be rooted in February.

To produce cascades, the shoot from the topmost leaf axil is grown on as the new leader, afterwards pinching all laterals as they form their fourth or fifth leaves. By the end of May or early in June the plants should be in their final 8- or 9-in. pots. When danger of frost has passed, stand the pots out-doors. Choose an open, sunny situation. Stand the plants on 'tabling' in front of a hedge or south-facing wall, preferably 4 ft or more from the ground.

Place a strong stake in each pot at an angle of 45° and secure a bamboo cane to it at an angle slightly off the perpendicular, pointing downwards. Along this, train the lead-ing shoots. Provide a firm 'shelf' on which the pots can stand. Fix some kind of framework or battens across the front to keep the pots from moving.

Drive a bamboo cane, up to 7 ft high, into the ground opposite each pot to which it should be tied. To prevent the leader from being broken, it should be gradually turned towards the support, by a loop of raffia and then tied every few inches as growth proceeds. Give liquid feeds at fourteen-day intervals until the flower buds begin to open. Stopping of all shoots should then cease.

Move the plants to the greenhouse in September, allowing the shoot to fall from the staging, and tie to wires stretched between battens on the floor and the staging, and thence to the rims of the pots. Well grown, the cascades of flowers will be 4 to 6 ft long.

If 'bushes' 3 to 4 ft high are required, give only one stop-ping when the plants are small. Flowering lasts from Oct-ober until December. When potting up, place the plants with a bud facing downwards. When the plant has taken hold in the new soil, the top is pinched back to the same second node, which then becomes the leader.

Charm Chrysanthemums have dainty single flowers

freely produced in many colours, the light dainty blooms making a welcome change from the usual types. Sow seed in January, pot on the young plants until they reach the 8 in. size, in which low mounds, 18 to 24 in. across, are covered with flowers. Separate colours available include white, yellow, apricot, red, and pink.

CHAPTER XI

CARNATIONS

THE CARNATION IS a highly hybridized creation belonging to the great and versatile genus *Dianthus*. Various kinds can be grown in the greenhouse, but none can compare with the 'Perpetual Flowering Carnation'. It is sometimes said that carnations are difficult to grow. This is not true provided we remember that they like lime, good soil, proper drainage, fresh air, light and freedom from pests. These are just the conditions appreciated by a large number of greenhouse plants. In addition, a moderate temperature of 50° is sufficient.

There is, of course, great beauty in other members of the dianthus family: the border carnation, the dainty alpine species, and the Sweet William. None of these bring the same joy and cheer during the dark winter days as the perpetual flowering varieties.

There are few other plants which bloom so continuously without showing signs of weakness. Should failures occur, they can usually be traced to inferior stock. Always buy your plants from a specialist grower.

To start a collection, it is best to buy plants in 3-in. pots. This is better than getting unrooted or even rooted cuttings, which are sometimes available. Established young plants will have been 'stopped' and will have several sturdy 'breaks'. Unless you have any special preferences, the choice of varieties can safely be left to the specialist supplier. If you have a low greenhouse, choose varieties of shorter habit. This does not necessarily mean shorter flower stems, for some varieties break low down on the stem.

Make sure carnations never become pot bound. Move them from the 3-in. pots to the 5-in. size and then to bigger pots according to growth. Always use clean pots, making sure they are dry.

Potting compost is most important. Although the John Innes Composts have been used with a measure of success, Mr. R. G. Allwood, of the world famous carnation firm, would never recommend them. His argument was that the peat in the composts is liable to turn acid as it decomposes and lime-loving carnations will not be at their best when this happens.

A suitable compost for carnations consists of 4 parts good loam, 1 part old manure and a quarter part of limestone chippings or mortar rubble. If the loam is heavy, add a little silver sand. To this mixture add a small amount of one of the carnation foods. Commercial growers use $\frac{1}{4}$ lb. to a barrow-load of mixture.

Carnations like firm potting but not so hard as to prevent water passing through the compost. Plants intended for winter flowering should be in their flowering pots by the end of June. At that time they can stand in a frame or other sheltered place outdoors, so long as they are sheltered from heavy rains and winds. This will lead to well ripened, mature stems for producing good flowers.

Avoid very wet or very dry root conditions at all times. Always give a good watering when necessary; frequent sprinklings are no good. Overhead syringings of water once a week are beneficial and helpful in keeping down pests. In hot weather, the greenhouse staging supporting the pots should be kept damp.

The 'stopping' of perpetual carnations has been made to sound complicated. Once it is understood it is an easy operation. It is simply removing the top of the growth to induce it to produce 'breaks', or side shoots, and so build up good shapely plants. We have to decide when and where to stop the plants. If a plant is not stopped at all, it will make long, straggly growth with one flower at the top. Plants must be in vigorous growing condition when stopped. If growth is too hard, fewer breaks will be made and therefore fewer flowers produced. Soft sappy growth, through being in poor light, should also be avoided.

It is best to carry out stopping between February and October. During the remainder of the year, breaks will be fewer and of poor quality. The correct way to stop a shoot is to break the lead out with a side bend. It can be done most easily early in the morning when growth is firm and brittle. It is not only the point of the stem which should be removed, for some of the developed leaves should be taken out as well. This means pinching out the top at the fifth or sixth joint. If all shoots on the plant are stopped at the same level, they should break evenly, thus producing a balanced flowering plant.

The stopping of the resulting breaks or side growths needs rather more care if the flowering season is to be prolonged. It is therefore advisable to stop the breaks at different times, to secure flowers over a lengthy period. The best plan is to look over the plants every few days and stop them as they are ready. As a guide, one may reckon that it will be five months from the time a shoot is stopped until the break produces a flower.

Greenhouse carnations need supports. They should be given at an early stage. While stakes and raffia are often used, it is best to provide good wire supports for each plant. There are various types available. A well supported plant will not only produce good, straight stems, with fine flowers, but there will be less trouble from split calyx. Well supported plants remain healthier than those allowed to flop about.

Do not leave the plants outdoors later than mid-August for it is better that flower buds should form under glass. From mid-September onwards, an occasional liquid feed will prove beneficial.

Always cut the flowers with long stems. In preparation for the second year's flowering, the plants should be moved to larger size pots in June or early July. While in some cases the quality of the flowers is not quite so good, the number of blooms produced is as great as from first year plants.

It is during the darkest days of winter that the perpetual flowering carnation is so valuable. Care is needed then, so that heat is not greatly increased, for high temperatures during dull weather are detrimental. It is better to keep the plants on the dry side during winter, giving water as and when really needed.

Taking a heel cutting

FIG. 8.

A certain amount of disbudding is necessary. This means plucking out the small buds that cluster near the terminal buds of each stem. Such disbudding results in larger though fewer blooms.

Propagation. Perpetual Flowering Carnations can be propagated by cuttings taken from December to March. Growths selected for cuttings should be of average size and taken half-way up the stem, where it is fairly thick with short inter-nodes. The cuttings should be about 3 in. long, having four pairs of leaves. These should be taken by cutting just below a thickened leaf-joint with a very sharp knife. Alternatively, a 'heel' cutting can be taken with a sharp downward pull and trimmed clean.

Sharp, washed, river sand is an ideal rooting medium. Vermiculite is sometimes used, as is a good compost mixture. The great thing is to keep the end of the cutting moist. It is not until roots have formed that nourishment is needed. Pluck off the lower leaves before inserting the cuttings; a quarter of an inch deep is enough. Plant the cuttings very firmly. Sometimes cuttings are dipped into a rooting hormone powder but this is certainly not necessary.

If you are rooting just a few cuttings, you can use a pot or pan. Larger quantities can be rooted on a bed made up on the bench, or staging. If a propagating case is available it will be of great help, especially if soil warming cables are in use. After five weeks or so, the cuttings will have rooted and can be moved into small pots. Do not bury the centres of the young plants.

It is also possible to raise Perpetual Flowering Carnations from seed. January and February are the best months for sowing, although it can be done throughout the spring and summer. Allow the seedlings to grow on without stopping them. The earliest plants will flower from July onward; inferior plants should be discarded by the end of September. The remainder can be potted on for future display.

Other Dianthus. Other types of dianthus can be grown in the small greenhouse. These include the perpetual Flowering Malmaisons, Border Carnations, Allwoodii (a beautiful group which is half carnation and half pink), the Chabaud and the so-called annual carnations. These will flourish in a cool or a cold greenhouse and will prolong the season.

There is a tremendous number of excellent varieties available and it is advisable to consult the catalogues of specialist growers, since new varieties are constantly being introduced.

Pests and Diseases. Keep a look-out for damage by thrips and footroot; see last Chapter.

CHAPTER XII

CACTI AND SUCCULENTS

CACTI AND SUCCULENTS are grouped together because they require very similar conditions. One of the main differences between them is that succulents are without spines. This is why they are sometimes preferred to cacti. Many genera can be grown where there is a minimum winter temperature of 45°. So long as there is ample ventilation, 70° and more during the summer will not harm these plants.

It is often said that cacti are desert plants and therefore need very little water. This is only partly true, for in their native home they are subjected to long spells of dry weather followed by periods of abundant rain. It is then the plants make new growth, extend their roots and store the water in their swollen stems, living on this reserve during the next dry period. It is this alternation of conditions that keeps the plants healthy and of good colour and robustness. In addition when 'at home' the plants receive the benefit of heavy dews. The thick skin and abundance of hairs found on many species give additional protection against great heat.

In greenhouses and living-rooms plants are more likely to be spoiled by over attention than neglect. It is wise to remember that in their natural conditions they often have to struggle for existence, which help to make them strong.

It is impossible to give precise directions for watering, for so much depends on the conditions under which the plants are grown. Many species have a covering of wax making them particularly decorative. It is when the plants are watered too freely that the leaves remain green instead of being an attractive glaucous shade.

The majority of the spring cacti require very little moisture during the winter – just enough to keep them from shrivelling. Succulents, however, need some watering although, even to these, extremely little should be given during December and January. Some succulents flower in the winter and vary in the times of their resting periods. The popular Christmas Cactus needs some water, in fact, if not enough moisture is obtained, the flower buds and even the segments may drop, as they often will when the temperature varies greatly.

The Lithops or 'Living Stones' have a natural resting period from early January until April. It therefore largely depends on the species being grown and the use of common sense as to when watering is done.

Whenever possible use rainwater, preferably with the chill off. If tap water has to be used, let it stand for some hours after being drawn, before applying it to the plants. It is important to make sure the plants have used up all the moisture in the soil before applying any more.

The first early spring watering should be done by standing the pots up to the rims in water. A soaking of this kind encourages new growth and will not usually need repeating until three or four weeks later. During June and July more water is needed, gradually slackening off in August and very little being given from October onwards. While the plants are growing well during the summer, they can be helped by giving occasional feeds of liquid manure.

The make-up of the potting mixture for cacti and succulents is not really critical. The John Innes No. 2 Compost is suitable or you can make up your own mixture on the following lines: 2 parts fibrous loam, 1 part each of fine leaf-mould, moistened peat and coarse silver sand. To these, add a good sprinkling of hoof-and-horn meal and superphosphate of lime, while a little sulphate of potash or seaweed fertilizer will be helpful.

Cacti are grown in ordinary flower pots or in glazed bowls. In the latter case, several different species can be grown together to give a good display. For this purpose, use species requiring similar conditions. Whether you buy a bowl of cacti or plant one up yourself, a good layer of crocks, pebbles or grit should be placed at the bottom. Then, when the surface soil appears dry, water can be applied and, with well drained compost, moisture will sink through the soil, any excess remaining among the drainage material, where the lower roots can use it. No more watering is necessary until the surface soil becomes dry again. If the surface remains wet for more than a week, either drainage is bad or too much water was given.

Apply water to the bowls with care. To avoid splashing the plants, use a can with a curved spout or a jug, so long as the bowls are not flooded.

When plants are grown in pots and a good porous soil mixture is used, they should remain in healthy condition for several years. All pots should have drainage material at the bottom. Grade this so that the bigger pieces are put in first. If a lump or two of charcoal can be added it will keep it all sweet. Coarse sand placed over the crocks is better than the peat moss sometimes used. If a plant has made much growth and is obviously too large for its pot, it should be moved to a bigger size with fresh compost.

When bought, succulent plants are usually in very small pots. Often they are seedlings or young plants from cuttings. Since the amount of soil in these small pots is so little, the nourishment it contains is soon used. In addition, the roots become restricted, affecting development. Also the amount of water a little pot can hold is very limited. It is therefore best to give the roots more room.

Many species and varieties benefit by being stood out in the rain during the summer. This not only freshens them but removes dust. An exception to this, however, is in the case of those kinds having a powdery or waxy 'bloom'. Water can easily spoil their appearance and, for these, it is best to use a small pair of bellows to blow off the dust.

Most cacti like plenty of light. Exceptions to this rule are the Christmas Cactus and the epiphyllums which prefer not to be in full sunlight. It is a good plan to turn the pots from time to time. This encourages even growth. Once flower heads show, however, do NOT turn the plants but leave them in position until the flowers are over.

Cacti and succulents like good ventilation but object to draughts. If kept in a close stuffy atmosphere, the plants become tired looking and of poor colour.

Whether grown in pots or bowls, cacti can be made more attractive as well as benefited by applying a top-dressing of coarse sand. This not only presents a natural looking ground for the plants, but also in summer checks evaporation, which is sometimes liable to be quite severe when the greenhouse atmosphere remains dry for any length of time.

The time to repot the plants is in the spring, when growth is becoming active. Move the plants gradually into large pots according to the growth they make. Since many species and varieties are spiny and difficult to handle, it is a good idea to place a strong paper collar around them. This makes it easier to move the plants properly. Canes should be pushed into the pots of taller growing specimens. Such support is almost essential for plants with rather fragile stems. Place the canes so that they are inconspicuous.

It is theoretically possible to raise from seed all cacti and succulents such as are grown in the greenhouse. Seed-raised plants are often better and stronger than plants propagated by means of cuttings. Most seedsmen offer seed in mixture, and this is quite an interesting way to secure a range of plants. Where seed of separate species is available one does know what to expect. Seed can be sown from the end of April until the beginning of August. In many cases germination is slow and erratic. Among species which germinate fairly rapidly are Cereus, Mammillaria and Echinocactus.

Where possible, the sowing should be done in a propagating case in the greenhouse. A temperature of not less than 70° is ideal. If such a case is not available germination will be slower. A simple seed-sowing compost consists of equal parts of horticultural peat and coarse silver sand. These should be rubbed through a fine sieve, afterwards adding a sprinkling of powdered charcoal. Seed pans up to 4 in. are better than pots for seed sowing. In these place an inch of drainage material, such as brick chips or broken crocks. Then add the compost, sow the seed very thinly and cover lightly with a mixture of silver sand and charcoal dust. Some of the seeds will be large enough to handle individually. The pans can be placed on shallow trays of water inside the propagation case. Cover the pans with paper until germination takes place. Given the right temperature and moisture, the growth should be seen within a week. Subsequently the young plants are moved singly into thumb size pots using a mixture of equal parts loam, peat, silver sand and small pieces of charcoal. From this time the plants will do well in a temperature around 65°.

Some species can be propagated by means of cuttings, particularly the perennial stemmed varieties. If cuttings are taken from a fairly soft part of the stem and are dried for two or three days they will usually root readily. If the stems are woody, rooting may be difficult.

The stemless varieties usually respond well to vegetative propagation. This includes *Zygocactus truncatus*. Cuttings of this consist of several stem segments. They are placed round the edge of 3- or 4-in. pots and, when rooted, are potted up individually. It is this species which used to be known as Phyllocactus – it is of a pendulous habit of growth, and is sometimes grafted on to an upright species, such as Pereskia, to make a standard plant.

Cacti and succulents are ideal as house plants and there is great pleasure to be had in growing a good selection of species in the greenhouse and using them as temporary living-room plants.

Since there is such a vast number available, we can only refer to a few of those suitable for growing in the small greenhouse. They include:

Cacti: *Aporocactus flagelliformis* (Rat's tail cactus), and various species of Echinocactus, Echinopsis, Epiphyllum, Mammillaria, Opuntia and Zygocactus.

Succulents: various species of Agave, Cotyledon, Crassula, Euphorbia, Kalanchoe (see Chapter VI), Lithops, Mesembryanthemum, Rochea, Sempervivum (house leeks), and Sedum.

CHAPTER XIII

EASY ORCHIDS

MANY AMATEUR GARDENERS believe that the growing of orchids is a difficult process, requiring a special greenhouse and equipment. This is not so. Neither is it essential to have a house exclusively for orchids. There are, of course, some exotic and very choice species which require special conditions but there are many that can be grown along with other plants in a mixed house.

In their native homes, most orchids grow on the fork of a tree or on rocks in a shady ravine, but they can certainly be cultivated in pots without difficulty. We are concerned here only with those species which are suitable for the amateur with a cool greenhouse in which a variety of plants are grown.

These species, which will be detailed later, will thrive in a minimum temperature of 45°. In fact, if the plants and their surroundings are kept dry, they will come to no harm where the temperature is several degrees lower. From June to September, therefore, they will succeed in the unheated greenhouse. Fresh air is needed but draughts are fatal.

Since in their native homes the plants are firmly fixed to a tree or rock, it is inadvisable to move them round as is usually done with other pot plants. When the temperature goes above 65° orchids like top ventilation, in preference to the greenhouse door being left open. Draughts must be avoided. Good drainage is needed and it is wise to stand the plants on inverted plant pots on a stage covered with ashes or gravel, or to use lath staging.

Shading is often required. Ideally, this should be provided by blinds fitted on the outside so that they can be pulled up and down according to weather conditions. Failing these, the glass can be stippled with whiting or Summer Cloud, while temporary blinds of muslin or similar material can be fixed on to the inside rafters. Shading must be gradually reduced as autumn advances.

A humid atmosphere is needed, particularly during spring and summer. It can be provided by damping down the plants and staging, a job which may have to be repeated several times during hot, sunny days. This should never be done late in the day or unwanted heavy moisture may remain on the plants through the night. The amount of damping during autumn and winter will depend on the temperature of the house.

From early May to September, plants need a lot of water. A thorough soaking should be given every five or six days. Do not dip the pot in water, for this expels the air from the compost, leading to an unwanted soggy condition. The sphagnum moss which should be kept on top of the pots is a good guide to water requirements. While it remains a bright green the plants have sufficient moisture, but once it becomes a greyish colour water is needed. Never give orchids more water when the compost is wet.

Less moisture is needed during autumn and winter. Water should be withheld for a short period during winter. This provides a 'rest' for the plants. Moisture given unnecessarily when roots are inactive can easily cause them to decay. Do not at any time apply water straight from the tap. Ideally it should be the same temperature as the greenhouse. This is where a tank inside the house is of advantage, particularly if rain water can be used. If plants are given a thorough soaking and extra damp moss is placed on and around the pots, they are unlikely to suffer harm if left for ten to fourteen days. This is a comfort when one is going on holiday, if there is no one to attend to the plants.

Orchids are remarkably free from pests and diseases. As an aid to keeping them in first-class condition the leaves should be sponged every five or six weeks with a good insecticide, preferably one with a derris base.

When bought from a specialist grower it is rarely necessary to repot for twelve months or so. Surface roots sometimes develop. This is not always an indication that the plants need more room. A little compost or additional moss can be placed on top of the pot. Even then, some strong surface roots may push up.

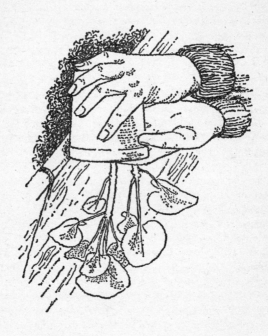

FIG. 9. Knocking out a plant for re-potting

The ordinary potting composts should not be used for orchids. Instead, special mixtures should be made up. The base of all these is osmunda fibre and sphagnum moss. The exact make-up of the mixture will depend on the species being grown and it is advisable to buy a suitable compost from a nurseryman or sundriesman who specializes in soils. Always tell him the group of orchids for which you need the mixture. Charcoal, coarse silver sand and peat are also used.

When repotting, fill the pot at least a quarter full of crocks placed upright for drainage. Then put in the plant, working the new compost in between the roots and around the collar, ramming it firm to hold the plant in position. Do not use large pots, those an inch or so bigger than the original size will be big enough. The best time for this job is from March to July, although Cypripediums can also be potted in February and Odontoglossums in September or March.

Many growers do not feed orchids at all, others apply manure or soot water to the floor of the greenhouse in a moist atmosphere, believing that growth is helped by the ammonia vapour. Orchids can, however, be helped by giving weak feeds of diluted dried blood or an infusion of bonemeal. These can be applied at monthly intervals from March to October.

A number of orchids can be raised from seed. Specialist orchid growers place seed in glass flasks, but the amateur gardener who wants to raise just a few plants, can sow seeds on the moss in which the plants are growing.

It is no use using an ordinary compost. Orchids have a special kind of fungus on their roots. Unless this is present in the compost, the plants will not thrive. When a plant is growing healthily this fungus is present. Therefore, seeds sown in such conditions will usually produce good plants. Simply sprinkle the seed around a growing plant. Do not water from overhead. It is best to stand the pots in a pan or pail of water and let moisture seep up to the surface. Applied from above, water may easily wash out the seed or cause it to become buried too deeply.

Germination is liable to be erratic. When the seedlings are growing nicely and have formed two or three leaves, they can be pricked out into small pots or a number can be placed around the edge of bigger pots. In either case, use a good orchid compost. Move to individual pots when they can be handled easily.

Orchids live a long time and well-grown plants will flower annually. Obviously much of the value of any orchid depends on its rarity and, in plants raised from seed, one should always look out for a new shade of colour or for any unusual, good habit.

Never be afraid of letting plants become large; in fact, too frequent dividing often reduces the number of flowers.

In deciding what species or varieties to grow, it is really best to consult a specialist grower. For a comprehensive book on the subject I recommend *Orchids and their Cultivation* by David Sanders. Membership of the Amateur Orchid Growers' Society will also be helpful and bring you in touch with other orchid lovers.

As a start in building up a little collection of orchids, the following can be recommended. One great point in their favour is that they will grow in a 'mixed house' and do not need to be alone, as do some species.

Calanthes regnieri, growing $2\frac{1}{2}$ ft high with white and rich pink flowers. There are several white or pink varieties and all flower in winter.

Cattleyas are most lovely orchids and among the easiest to manage are *C. bowringiana* with rosy-purple flowers in October. *C. mendelii,* rosy-lilac and purple in spring. *C. skinneri,* pink, purple and white flowers in May. All grow 10 to 12 in. high and there are many hybrids.

Coelogyne cristata and its varieties are splendid for winter flowering. The rather straggly plants look best in shallow pans where the flowers, 6 to 9 in. high, appear from February to April.

Cymbidiums are a little more difficult to grow, but there are many really beautiful cymbidiums that ought to be in even the smallest collection of orchids. Many of these can be had in colour from November to May. The flowers are particularly long lasting and it is not unknown for them to remain in good condition for more than two months.

Cypripedium flowers are much used in bouquets, corsages and buttonholes. The colour range takes in almost all shades except blue. Do not cut the flowers until they have been open for at least a week. It is best to take the advice of your supplier as to what you can grow, since this will depend upon your growing facilities, but *Cypripedium insigne* with white, purple and brown flowers and its many varieties and hybrids, can always be depended upon.

Pleiones are excellent for the small unheated greenhouse. They are easy to grow, not expensive, and require very little room. *P. formosana* (or *P. pricei*), pale lilac and white, has individual flowers about 2½ in. in diameter.

Any necessary dividing of the bulbs can be done after flowering or during the dormant season. It is not difficult to detach pseudo-bulbs which can be potted up separately. The plants are moved to larger pots and growth develops. Seen in the so-called half-pots, say, 8 in. in diameter, pleiones give an imposing display.

CHAPTER XIV

GREENHOUSE CLIMBERS AND TRAILERS

CLIMBERS FROM SEED – TRAILING PLANTS

THERE ARE MANY climbing plants which are excellent for growing in the greenhouse or in a glazed porch, where they will become more or less a permanent feature. The type of plants which can be grown will depend upon the size of the house.

Climbing or semi-climbing subjects are always attractive, so that this class of plant does require special consideration. Among these, *Lapageria rosea* is a most glorious evergreen climber from Chile. Its flowers have been described as waxen lilies, and are of a beautiful shade of rose-crimson, while there is an attractive white form. A good soil mixture, free from lime, and some shade from full sun are its needs.

Not perhaps the easiest of plants to manage, Mutisia decurrens also from South America, is another handsome climbing subject. Once established, it will produce its heads of large, bright, orange-scarlet flowers, each one being from 4 to 6 in. in diameter. The glaucous-green leaves terminate in a tendril enabling the plant to climb up wire or other supports. Warmth and sunshine suits mutisias of which there are several species, although some shade from the brightest sun is desirable.

Plumbago capensis is first class and very easy indeed. If established plants are kept cut back to the hard wood annually, a real sheet of Cambridge blue will be obtained. The white form, alba is also excellent. A winter temperature of 40° is sufficient, and in the summer plenty of air is needed. It can be propagated from early cuttings. A fairly rich, well drained site is needed for best results.

Stephanotis floribunda is a real beauty that does require warmer conditions. Its small white, scented, tubular flowers, are very showy and the foliage also is ornamental. It likes good rooting conditions, and can be propagated from cuttings started in heat.

Solandra grandiflora is an attractive climbing plant for a warm greenhouse with a winter temperature of around 45°. Sometimes known as the Peach-coloured Trumpet Flower, it freely produces, during March and April, fragrant, greenish-white blooms which gradually turn to a brownish-yellow. It requires light sunshine and ample moisture during the growing season, and does best in a well drained sandy loam.

Cantua buxifolia is an elegant, much-branched flowering plant of easy cultivation. It can be grown as a shrub but is seen at its best trained up the roof or on a pillar in the cool greenhouse. The leaves are slightly downy and during April and May, terminal clusters of five to eight long, funnel-shaped flowers are produced. In the bud stage, they are bright red, but open rosy-red, suffused yellow on the tube.

It thrives in a mixture of turfy loam, leaf-mould and silver sand and may be kept in a large pot but is happiest when planted out in the greenhouse border. Propagation is from cuttings of half ripened wood, rooting them in sandy soil in a close atmosphere.

Jasminum primulinum is a greenhouse relative of the popular outdoor jasmine, with similar yellow flowers that adorn the greenhouse in winter. It can be trained on a wall or up the rafters and needs no more than 45°. *J. revolutum* flowers from June to August. Both will grow in pots or the border and like plenty of water in spring and summer. Propagation is from cuttings of firm shoots from April to August.

Passion Flower. *Passiflora caerulea* is one of the most beautiful climbing plants, having delicately wrought floral parts that have been described as representing Our Lord's Passion. It is almost hardy and in a greenhouse needs a winter temperature of no more than 40°, but plenty of sun in summer. The variety 'Constance Spry' is white.

Rose. Two famous old climbers are splendid adornments of the greenhouse that is not too small. One is Maréchal Niel, a beautifully formed, soft gold, highly scented variety. The other is the white Climbing Niphetos, now not so easy to get.

Streptosolen jamesonii is an attractive climber for the cool house, producing orange-scarlet flowers in clusters during the summer. It grows well either in pots or the greenhouse border, but naturally it grows larger where the roots are unrestricted. Propagation is by cuttings taken during the summer and rooted in silver sand.

Climbers from Seed

A number of really interesting, climbing plants can be raised from seed very easily. The following can be used for the back of a lean-to greenhouse or to cover pillars or temporary supports.

Cardiospermum halicacabum. Easier to remember by its common name of Balloon Vine, this is an interesting, rapid-growing climber from the tropics. It succeeds in a winter temperature of 45° and, although a perennial, it is best treated as an annual. It can be sown in autumn or spring and, after pricking out the seedlings, three plants can be put into an 8-in. pot, to make a delightful display.

Cobaea scandens. Sometimes known as the Cup-and-Saucer vine. The Canterbury bell type of flowers of a deep velvety-purple colour, 'sit' on short, stubby stems. The large seeds germinate most freely when sown on edge, in gentle heat, in either pots or boxes, of well drained compost. An easy one.

Gourds. These are interesting and attractive during the summer and autumn. They like a warm, fairly humid atmosphere. *Cucumis anguria*, the gooseberry gourd, has many fruits of gooseberry shape and size, and the Lagenaria varieties have fruits of various shapes, which give rise to the common names such as bottle, pipe, serpent and spoon gourds. Sow seeds singly in small pots in the greenhouse. After germination, the plants grow quickly. Support them at an early stage and train them up the sides or back of the greenhouse and on to the inside of the rafters. Some of the foliage can be removed to prevent the greenhouse becoming shaded by the plants.

Ipomaea. Often known as Morning Glories and closely resembling the convolvulus, they are of easy culture. Specially good is *I. rubro-coerulea*, particularly the beautiful variety Heavenly Blue. Other good varieties include: Cardinal, bright orange-scarlet; Flying Saucers, sky-blue marked with white; Hearts and Honey, salmon-orange tipped gold; and Wedding Bells, soft lavender-mauve with whitish-yellow throat. Seed germinates evenly if soaked in water overnight or if lightly chipped before sowing in a temperature of 60°.

Maurandia barclaiana. Another climbing plant which thrives in a fairly low winter temperature. The much branched shoots and small green leaves, when against a wall, lie quite flat. The shoots have a tendency to trail as well as climb and make a charming drape for the greenhouse staging. The violet-blue speckled flowers are soon over but are freely produced. A perennial plant, it will flower in the first year from a spring sowing.

Thunbergia alata is a half-hardy perennial usually treated as an annual. Known as Black-eyed Susan and the Clock Vine, it has twining stems up to 4 ft in length. The dark green, almost triangular, leaves have cut edges and each pale yellow flower has a deep purple 'eye'. Sow seed $\frac{1}{8}$ in. deep in a temperature of 65°.

Tropaeolum peregrinum. The Canary Creeper, looks well seen growing up a pillar or other support. The canary-yellow flowers are prettily fringed. A rich soil can lead to luxuriant foliage which hides the blooms. Use ordinary good compost and feed the plants when flowers show.

Trailing Plants

These can be grown in hanging baskets or suspended from the greenhouse beams in boxes. They can also be grown on the staging where they present a pleasing effect.

The natural trailing habit of the ivy-leaved pelargoniums, makes them indispensable. They flower through the summer and, if there is warmth, they will often bloom in winter too. The old-fashioned variety Madame Crousse remains good and others are listed in Chapter VI.

Some fuchsias have a spreading and trailing habit, and can be trained against a wall or fixed to greenhouse rafters, where the flowers will hang down, and produce a fine display.

Several of the abutilons or Indian Mallows, look splendid in baskets, having bell-like flowers which hang on short stems from the leaf axils.

Pendulus, tuberous-rooted begonias are also fine for hanging baskets, or for draping the staging. They can be raised in the same way as the show begonias, as described in Chapter VIII. When growing nicely, transfer them directly to baskets or the staging. For winter flowering, the fibrous-rooted begonias, such as the splendid Gloire de Lorraine, are most effective. For these, rather more heat is required.

Achimenes are useful trailing plants dealt with in Chapter VIII.

Lachenalias are also excellent for basket work. These too, can be placed so that they grow from the sides of the baskets as well as the top. Plant in August under cool conditions. Of the many handsome colours available, the most reliable is *Lachenalia nelsonii* (*L. aloides*) producing greenish-yellow marked scarlet, flowers.

Campanula isophylla produces a profusion of bright blue blooms over a long period from August onwards. Seen at its best where growths are allowed to fall over the sides of the container. There are also lilac-blue and white forms.

Tradescantia is a well-known trailing plant. The green varieties are not so attractive as the variegated forms.

Zebrinas are often confused with tradescantias but require warmer conditions. *Z. purpusii* is specially good, having reddish-purple leaves. Both are readily increased from cuttings.

Columnea aurantiaca, with bright orange flowers, is lovely in baskets. *Saxifrage sarmentosa* is known as Mother of Thousands, since it produces many fresh plantlets. The green form is ornamental, but the variety *tricolor* has leaves beautifully blotched with cream and crimson.

Ferns of various kinds look well in baskets, especially *Asparagus plumosus* and *Asparagus sprengeri*, while the dainty growth of the Selaginellas is delightful.

CHAPTER XV

POT-GROWN FRUIT TREES

IT IS UNLIKELY that any gardener would buy a small green-house solely for growing fruit trees. Even so, there is no reason why anyone should not cultivate a few specimens under glass. Provided the right varieties are selected and they are treated properly, not only will fruit be available but also the trees will be ornamental and an evidence of the grower's skill.

No staging is needed; the pots can stand on a hard base on the greenhouse floor. The house for pot fruits can be un-heated or heated only sufficiently to exclude frost during the flowering period and for a few weeks afterwards. This is the stage at which there is the greatest attention needed. Then regular early morning syringing with water will keep pests away. Continual spraying whenever the weather is bright greatly aids the ripening fruit.

One advantage of growing pot fruit is that after the crop has been gathered, the pots can be stood outdoors if possible plunged in weathered coal ashes. This both encourages the production of fruit buds for the following year and allows the greenhouse to be filled with colourful flowering plants during the winter months.

There are two ways of starting to grow pot fruit. For quick results, you can buy four-year-old trees from a specialist grower. Some supply trees already in pots, in which case it will be wise to remove the top 2 or 3 in. of soil and replace it with fresh rich compost.

It is essential to buy trees on the right stock. Apples should be on East Malling IX, pears on Angers Quince or Quince A. Peaches on peach or Mussell stock and plums on Mussell. The subject is highly technical and a specialist fruit nursery

should be consulted. Grapes and figs are grown on their
own roots from cuttings or, in the case of grapes, from
eyes.

If you do not mind waiting for a crop, you can buy maiden
or year-old specimens more cheaply. These can be put into
18-in. size pots, using a compost such as the John Innes No. 2.
Avoid using too much sand, otherwise the compost may
dry out quickly during summer. Trim back bruised or
broken roots, cutting them in such a way that the root
system fits into the pot without cramping. Avoid cutting the
fibrous roots. Place plenty of crocks at the bottom of the
pots to prevent waterlogging. Carefully work the soil among
the roots. Tapping the bottom of the pot on the bench as the
job proceeds ensures contact between soil and roots and
prevents air pockets.

Potting is best done in autumn, no pruning of top growth
being done until the following February, when the roots are
starting into action. For the first year the pots can be left
plunged outdoors, any flower buds being nipped off as soon
as seen. In subsequent years, they should be taken into the
greenhouse each January. While there the trees should be
sprayed with water on all fine days to encourage growth.

Trees in pots can be grown as bushes or shaped single
cordons, which are easy to manage, but fan-shaped and
espalier specimens need more attention. The development
of the trees is controlled by disbudding which takes the place
of summer pruning. If you grow figs, remember they love
lime, so add some to the potting mixture.

The best temperature for pot fruit is 45° in daytime and
55° to 60° at night. Routine sprayings of insecticides and
fungicides should keep the trees clean.

There is a wide choice of suitable varieties and we must
bear in mind the question of pollination. The following
apples can be relied upon for good crops. Dessert apples:
James Grieve, Ellison's Orange, Ribston Pippin and Cox's
Orange Pippin. The latter will not fruit, however, unless one
of the first two are growing with it. If you fancy a cooking

apple, try Newton Wonder (December–April) and Peasgood Nonsuch (October–December).

For pears, two or more of the following should be grown. William's Bon Chrétien (September), Louise Bonne of Jersey (October), Doyenne du Comice (November–December) and Winter Nelis (December–March).

Cherries and plums are rather difficult, needing skilled culture and a greenhouse that is not too small. Peaches (best variety, Peregrine) and nectarines (variety John Rivers), though requiring also to be fan-trained, are less difficult, but need a fair expanse of glass. Figs lend themselves well to pot cultivation and really good varieties include Brown Turkey and White Marseilles.

The best variety of **grape** for pot culture is Black Hamburgh. You will be able to buy a one-year specimen in a 5- or 6-in. pot. It will need moving to a 12-in. pot, using J.I. No. 3 or a similar compost. Insert two upright 4-ft canes, one on each side of the pot and join their tops by a horizontal cane. Then train the vine up one cane, across the top and down the other cane, eventually forming a 'hoop'. Regulate the lateral shoots so they are not less than 10 to 12 in. apart. Pinch out the growing point of each lateral one leaf beyond the first embryo bunch of grapes as it forms, and limit the number of bunches on each vine to six.

Grape vines can be started into growth at different times. In heat you can start in November for ripe fruit in April, in December for May and in January for June ripening. In the cool house fruit can be had in July by starting the plants in March. Without any heat, vines started in March will produce fruit in August and September.

Ripe **strawberries** from late April onwards are a luxury indeed. Forcing the plants is not difficult in any way. Royal Sovereign is the best variety for forcing and one-year-old pot-plants should be used. It is possible to buy these in September. If, however, you grow your own strawberry plants for normal outdoor cropping, you should select young plants in August or September. They should be planted early before winter weather sets in. About the middle of March these plants are fed with bonemeal at 2 to 3 oz. to the sq. yd. of bed. When the flowers begin to develop in these selected plants, they should be removed to encourage the development of strong runners. Three-inch pots of good compost should then be prepared and inserted beside the row of plants. Place them so that the top of each pot is at ground level.

As the runners reach the pots, they should be pegged in, using wire or wooden pegs. Once it is evident that the plants are well rooted, the runners should be severed from the parent plants. After ten days or so they can be moved to the 5-in. pots in which they will fruit. Firm planting is advisable and, after standing in semi-shade for a week or so, the pots should be placed on a hard base in full sun.

During summer, give frequent syringings of water as well as liquid manure. Towards the end of October lay the pots on their sides and about the second week in November move them to the cold frame against a sheltered wall, keeping the crowns of the plants pointing outwards.

In early January take the pots into the greenhouse where there is a temperature of 40° to 45° at night. Since strawberries should be forced gently until the flowers open, it is best to keep a day temperature of not much more than 50°. In February the top soil should be removed from the pots and be replaced with rich compost. When the plants are growing well syringe them frequently.

Once the plants are in full flower the day temperature can go up to 65° and, as long as the plants are hand fertilized, using a camel's-hair brush or rabbit's tail, the fruit should set well.

If the plants show signs of fruiting heavily they should be thinned. Allow twelve to fifteen berries from each pot. As a rule, the trusses hang quite clear of the soil, but it may be necessary to insert twiggy sticks so that the berries are fully exposed to light. As the berries begin to swell, the temperature can be raised to 70° or even more during daytime, although it will be less at night. Keep the pots well watered but stop overhead syringing once the berries begin to colour, although liquid manure may still be given at seven-day intervals.

Strawberries are very susceptible to the botrytis disease. See last Chapter.

For melons and rhubarb, see the chapter on vegetables.

CHAPTER XVI

OUT-OF-SEASON VEGETABLES

ALTHOUGH THE MAJORITY of glasshouses are used for ornamental plants, several vegetables can profitably be grown. The intensity and duration of light has a marked effect on the time taken by vegetable crops to mature.

Lettuces can be sown from September onwards, the earliest sowings being ready in December. October sowings will mature in February. For cutting in March, sow at the end of October, putting the plants in their final positions in December.

For heated houses, suitable varieties are: Amplus, Cheshunt Early Giant, Cheshunt 5B, Proeftuins Blackpool and Cannington Forcing. Sow in boxes, later pricking off the seedlings into other boxes. Seed can also be sown in the greenhouse border. A suitable sowing temperature is between 55° and 60° decreasing it by 10° after germination. When grown on the greenhouse floor or bench, the plants should be spaced 7 in. apart.

Look out for botrytis, especially in winter (see last Chapter).

Peas can be cultivated in pots or the greenhouse border. For pots, rely on dwarf varieties, such as Kelvedon Wonder and Little Marvel, which can be sown in December for an early crop. Ten-inch pots are big enough to take six seeds. Sow them 1½ in. deep around the inside edge of clean, well-crocked pots, which should be filled to rather more than two-thirds of their depth. Use a mixture of 3 parts good fibrous loam and 1 part each of leaf-mould or peat, and silver sand. Work in some hydrated lime, although crushed builders' rubble is better.

After sowing, water the pots and stand them on a shelf near the glass. As growth proceeds fill the pots gradually with more compost. Avoid high temperatures, keeping heat to 65° during the day, with 10° lower at night.

For border culture, provided the soil is good, simply fork over the ground, working in a dressing of bonemeal at the rate of 3 to 4 oz. to the sq. yd. Sow during December and January, in drills about 2 in. deep, either in single rows or staggered. Provide twiggy sticks at an early stage, and as growth develops, suitable supports should be used.

Occasional overhead sprayings are beneficial. If the soil is moist before sowing, it will not need watering very frequently. Keep the temperature from rising above 65°, and avoid draughts. A close, dry atmosphere encourages red spider. Full light and plenty of fresh air are needed to maintain healthy, productive growth.

Radishes can be grown successfully in the greenhouse so long as there are adequate supplies of organic matter in the soil. On poor soils that dry out easily, radishes tend to become hard, stringy and hot flavoured. They dislike a close, hot atmosphere. Sow in deep boxes or on the glasshouse bench or in the greenhouse 'floor' soil. In the latter case seed can be broadcast. Alternatively, sow in rows 3 in. apart, making sure the soil is moist.

Only moderate heat is necessary, and if the light is reasonably good, a temperature of 45° to 50° should be suitable. Water is rarely necessary or desirable. Short-topped forcing varieties are best for glass production, particularly the forcing strain of French Breakfast, Sparkler and other turnip-shaped varieties.

Mint can be brought into the greenhouse for winter production. It can be grown in boxes or large pots, or on the greenhouse floor. The roots should be laid flat in little trenches about 3 in. deep, and are best started under cool conditions. Once growth is seen, a temperature of 50° will be suitable. When growing nicely, a few, fine, mist sprays of water will provide the atmosphere liked by these plants, and it should be possible to cut shoots over a long period.

Beans, Dwarf French. These can be grown in pots or

boxes in the cool greenhouse. For this purpose, it is best to use 9- or 10-in. pots which are well crocked and filled with a compost of the John Innes No. 2 type. Fill the pots to three parts of their depth, and space seven or eight beans around the edge of the pot, covering them with $1\frac{1}{2}$ in. of soil. Subsequently, the number of plants can be reduced to four or five.

Lightly syringe the plants at frequent intervals. This not

FIG. 10. Showing the crocks for drainage purposes

only ensures that the flowers set well but keeps down red spider. Once the pods have set, it is a good plan to apply liquid manure at ten-day intervals. To keep the plants upright, place twiggy sticks in the pots. The aim should be to maintain a temperature of 55° or so, although no harm is done if it rises a little during the daytime. The plants appreciate fresh air but not draughts.

Varieties: Masterpiece and The Prince, both having long fleshy pods of good flavour.

Beans, Climbing French. These have all the merits of the dwarf type, but usually give a heavier yield. Sow in the greenhouse border and train on wires or strings. Raise them in pots in the same way as the dwarf beans, sowing from late January onwards.

If one seed is sown in each small pot, it avoids a check when transplanting to final positions, at 9 or 10 in. apart. While the plants will often climb up the strings or wires of their own accord, it is a good plan to give one or two ties to keep growths upright. Avoid soggy root conditions, although the plants will need watering from time to time. Once the flowers have set, liquid manure will be helpful. Syringe the plants occasionally to keep down red spider.

Variety: Tender and True, also known as the Guernsey Runner, is of most delicious flavour.

Chicory. For earliest forcing, lift plants from the open ground in October; later batches can be brought in as required. Immediately after lifting, dry off the roots for a few days, so they receive a temporary check to growth.

To prepare them for forcing, cut off top growth to within an inch of the crown. Shorten the roots to a uniform length of about 8 in. and reject all fanged specimens.

Where small quantities are concerned, and space is limited, three or four can be planted in big pots of sandy soil free from pebbles. A similar sized pot is then inverted on the top. Place these pots where there is a temperature of 45° to 50°. Planted in the greenhouse soil, the trimmed chicory is placed upright about 18 in. deep.

Roots can also be planted similarly in deep boxes. Occasionally a covering of fermenting manure is applied to give forcing conditions, though if planting is done in the heated glasshouse, this is not necessary. Heavy soil, bad drainage and excessive heat are the things to avoid.

Cucumbers. These can be grown and supported in pots, but when in the greenhouse border, some means of support by wires, canes or string will be needed. A night temperature of not less than 65° is required. Where this cannot be provided, do not sow the seed too early.

Place the seed edgeways, ½ in. deep, in J.I. Seed Compost,

providing bottom heat if possible. Cover with glass and paper, removing them when germination occurs. After a fortnight, move the seedlings to 3-in. pots of J.I. Compost No. 2 keeping it moist but not wet. Subsequently, move to larger pots or to a prepared bed.

Prepare a well drained bed, which must not become hard and airless. Layers of strawy manure and good soil make the best bed. Cucumbers like a close, moist atmosphere, although in early summer the ventilators should be opened occasionally.

Syringing with water at midday and frequent damping down helps growth. Once the plants are growing well, they will need training up wires or other supports. Stop the lateral shoots after the second leaf and the resulting sub-laterals also.

Cucumbers often throw out white roots on the surface. This is an indication that a top-dressing is needed. Straw or strawy manure can be used; some days after it has been put on give a dressing of very rich soil. Shade is needed during hot weather, but it should not be too dense. Sufficient water should always be available, but too much is definitely harmful.

Beware botrytis (see last Chapter).

Varieties: Butcher's Disease Resisting, immune to spot disease, and a heavy cropper. Conqueror, dark green, long fruits of good shape. Telegraph, a reliable heavy cropper.

Melons. Sow from early January onwards, using clean, 3-in. pots of J.I. Compost. Two seeds in each pot should be covered with a quarter inch of soil, and the stronger seedling subsequently left. In a temperature of 65° germination will be rapid.

Plunge the sown pots up to their rims in peat, leaf-mould or light soil, preferably on bottom heat. Cover with glass and brown paper. When the plants are 3 in. high, move to 5-in. pots and spray frequently with water.

While melons can be fruited in large pots, it is better to plant them in the greenhouse border. Allow 18 in. between each plant and provide support to keep the plants upright.

Melons are subject to collar rot, so that moisture should be kept from the centre of the plant and from settling around the stems.

Take out the growing point to encourage side shoots. Three or four laterals can be taken and tied to wires on each side of the stem, but all others should be removed. Pollen can be transferred from the male flowers by means of a camel's-hair brush or rabbit's tail. The best time for this job is about midday, preferably when the weather is sunny.

Beware of botrytis (see last Chapter).

Mustard and Cress can be sown in pots, boxes or on the greenhouse staging soil, according to the quantity required. Sow little and often, using a good compost made fairly firm and watered well.

When the surface moisture has drained off, sow the seed fairly thickly, lightly pressing it in. Do not cover with soil but apply brown paper to provide darkness, or stand the boxes in a dark position for a few days.

So that they mature together, sow the cress four days before the mustard. The latter will germinate within three or four days, and both should be ready for cutting within seven or eight days.

Rhubarb. For forcing in the greenhouse, three-year-old crowns are best. These should be lifted and left on the surface of the ground for a week or more so that they first become exposed to the air and frost.

Roots, with crown exposed, should be packed closely together on a layer of good soil, under the greenhouse staging. Deep boxes may also be used, and if a mat or something similar is hung in front of the staging, this will exclude the light, and encourage good results.

Give a light watering and provide a temperature of about 45°. After a week or ten days, this may be increased to 55°, but do not allow it to get much beyond this, or the sticks will become flabby. Sticks should be ready for pulling five weeks after forcing is commenced, each stick being completely drawn away from the plant without damaging it.

Most varieties of rhubarb may be forced, but the naturally earlier kinds are most suitable; Prince Albert matures most quickly of all, followed by Hawke's Champagne, The Sutton and Victoria.

Tomatoes. Growing tomatoes out of doors is a chancy business, so that even a small greenhouse is of great advantage in producing a crop of fruit. The greenhouse also enables you to raise from seed varieties that are superior in flavour to those sold in the shops.

Seed can be sown from January onwards according to the amount of heat available. If a temperature of 55° to 60° cannot be provided, it is best to wait until March before sowing or to buy plants in pots in April.

The earliest sowings will produce ripe fruit from the end of April onwards. It is also possible to have a crop during the autumn from an early summer sowing, so long as plants are in position in July.

Cleanliness is very important and all pots and boxes, as well as the compost itself, must be free from pests and diseases. The J.I. Seed Compost is quite suitable for sowing, although it is easy to make up a mixture of loam and peat, with a good sprinkling of coarse silver sand.

It is advisable to bring the compost into the greenhouse a few days before use so that it warms through before sowing. Make the compost in the pots or boxes fairly firm, paying attention to the corners and edges. The seed is large and can be sown singly.

If up to an half inch is allowed between the seeds, it will enable the young plants to develop without becoming 'drawn' and leggy and will also make it easier for pricking out. Cover the seed with about an eighth of an inch of compost. Then place glass and paper over the trays. Turn the glass daily to prevent drips from condensation.

Tomato seed germinates very quickly and the coverings must not be kept on after growth is seen, otherwise the seedlings will be spoilt. During this period, the temperature should remain around 60°. Do not let the compost dry out.

A fairly moist atmosphere will be helpful but, when the outside temperature is low, avoid overwatering and do not water late in the day.

The seedlings can be pricked out as soon as the first rough or true leaf appears. They must be handled with great care. Lift them by the leaves to prevent damage to the little stems. Pot moderately firmly so that excessive water can drain away easily. Use the J.I. No. 2 mixture, or something similar. The plants must not be forced into growth, since short-jointed specimens are required. These can be encouraged by good light, moderate temperature and a fairly dry atmosphere, which means giving attention to ventilation. Give the plants more room as they develop and usually they will be in 5-in. pots within a matter of five weeks from the time of sowing.

The modern method of growing tomatoes is by 'ring culture'. By this system the plant develops two root zones – one by which it drinks and the other by which it is fed. Superior quality crops are produced without the constant watering that tomatoes otherwise need when they are growing away fast. Susceptibility to disease is reduced.

Make up a bed, 5 in. deep, of small, washed gravel or of household ashes, free of dust, which have been weathered out of doors for a month. This bed can be either in the greenhouse border or on the bench if a water-holding trough 6 in. deep is erected on it. Water the bed thoroughly.

On this bed stand a number of bottomless cylinders, about 9 in. in diameter and 7 to 8 in. deep. Bituminized paper 'rings' are sold for the purpose, but any non-porous material, including tins with the bottoms cut out, will serve.

Fill the ring firmly with J.I. No. 3 Compost to within 1½ in. of the top. Water the tomato seedlings, then transplant them into the rings, one plant in each, and give a thorough watering to the ring.

From then onwards keep the bed thoroughly well watered, but give *no water to the ring* except such as is necessary for applying a liquid fertilizer. This must be of a sort specially designed for tomatoes, with a high potash content; the usual application is at the rate of one tablespoonful in $2\frac{1}{2}$ pints of water once a week, but it should not be given until the first truss of fruit begins to set.

Provide stout canes or stakes for the support of the plants and tie them up with raffia or very soft string. Persistently pluck out the side-shoots that sprout in the leaf-axils – the angle between the main stem and a leaf-stalk. 'Stop' the main stem when five or six trusses have developed. Provide some shade in periods of hot sun. Overhead syringing with water encourages a good set of fruit.

The more traditional methods are to grow the plants in the greenhouse border, or in large pots or in deep boxes that give the plants a good root area of not less than 10 in. × 10 in. × 10 in. Crock pots and boxes thoroughly. Water rather sparingly at first but copiously and *regularly* after the fruit begins to set. A spell of drought followed by a flooding may cause the fruit to split. Feed with a tomato fertilizer.

Tomatoes are the victims of several ailments, such as botrytis (see last Chapter), but several of its troubles are due to faulty cultivation. 'Blossom-end rot' results from lack of water, 'greenback' from either too little potash or too much sun, 'dry set' from too dry an atmosphere, preventing the fruit from forming.

Varieties. Raising from your own seed enables you to grow varieties with the qualities that really matter for the amateur – flavour. The seedlings sold in markets are herein indifferent, though Moneymaker is not bad. So choose Ailsa Craig or Alicante, Eurocross 'A' and Golden Queen.

CHAPTER XVII

GREENHOUSE ENEMIES

PESTS – DISEASES

SUCCESS IN THE cultivation of greenhouse plants is greatly dependent upon cleanliness, and it pays to look over plants frequently to ensure that they remain in good condition. There are various pests and diseases which may attack plants, and it is advisable to make oneself familiar with the possibilities. They vary in their method of attack, and because of this, need to be dealt with in different ways. The first need is to distinguish between a disease and an insect pest.

There is ample proof that a healthy plant is capable of resisting many of the troubles which ordinarily attack weak plants. Specimens in poor condition often allow diseases and pests to gain a hold. This is one good reason for not retaining any plant which is in other than good order.

Rubbish should be kept from accumulating beneath the greenhouse staging or in odd corners, for this provides a breeding place for many pests. Woodwork, glass, pots, boxes and tools should all be kept clean. Some greenhouses have an inside tank and it is quite easy for such water holders to hold impure water which is another frequent cause of trouble.

Pests

Insect pests can be divided into two groups – those which bite or chew, and those which suck, the suckers include aphides (especially green and black fly) which attack all types of plants. They breed very quickly and it is therefore essential to deal with them immediately they are noticed, for delay of a day or two will lead to a tremendous increase.

Aphis. Fortunately, there are very many methods of getting rid of aphides and a number of quite safe insecticides, many with a Derris base, are usually effective in the forms of sprays or dusts. Fumigation is perhaps an even better means of dealing with these green, black and white flies. There are many so-called 'smoke bombs' which if used rightly, do the job for which they are intended, without harming the plants. The manufacturer's directions, however, should be read carefully, as there are plants allergic to fumigants.

One of the problems of spraying is that so often it is done only on the top leaves, whereas the pests are on the under-sides of the leaves or safely settled in the centre of the plant. Fairly forceful sprays should be applied under the leaves and at the growing point. One of the undesirable features of green fly attack is that they excrete a sticky honeydew, on which there often develops a fungus known as 'sooty mould'.

The presence of green aphides also encourages **ants,** which feed on the honeydew. Therefore ants must also be destroyed and a ready means of getting rid of them is to dust their runs and suspected nesting places with naphthalene or with one of the several proprietary ant powders. Ants are more likely to be present where the soil becomes very dry under the staging, so that occasional sprays of water there will do good.

Cuckoo spit or **frog hopper** is often a nuisance. The frothy spittle surrounds a tiny grub which feeds on the juices of plants and exudes the froth as a means of protection. Hand-pick this pest, and then spray the plants with a strong insecticide.

Eelworm is a microscopic creature that works invisibly. It is difficult to diagnose, but any kind of stunting, distortion or thickening is a reason for suspecting eelworm. There are many species of eelworm, each attacking one particular genus. Chrysanthemums, daffodils, phloxes and potatoes are among the most susceptible. Treatment is difficult for the amateur and the only thing to do is to uproot and burn the whole plant before others are attacked.

Leaf-miner is a tiny grub that tunnels its way within the tissue of a leaf, leaving wriggly channellings, as in the chrysanthemum, or blisters, as in celery. The grub is at the extremity of the channelling. Pinch it there and spray the plants with a BHC insecticide or fumigate the whole house with a BHC smoke.*

Mealy bug is a tiny, whitish, waxy, bug-like creature that lays its eggs in a surround of woolly material. In a very short time the whole plant can easily become spoiled. It will attack many kinds of plants and is one of the most difficult pests to dislodge. Rub off the pests with a soft cloth or paper and fumigate with BHC or nicotine. Vines are very susceptible; apply methylated spirit to the rods with a stiff brush in winter.

Red Spider is a serious greenhouse pest. It is a minute creature – to the naked eye a mere dot of rust. It feeds on the undersides of leaves, which assume a grey, mottled appearance. It is encouraged by hot, dry conditions, and its presence is often noticed by greyish leaf markings. A humid atmosphere should be provided, since the pests cannot thrive in this. Fumigate with azobenzine smoke.

Thrips. Another menace. It may attack a wide range of plants, including carnations, begonias, gloxinias, streptocarpus and foliage plants. They are thin, visible, fast-moving yellow or black. Leaves and stems become streaked and distorted. Flower buds turn brown. Fumigate with nicotine shreds. Thrips like the same conditions as red spiders.

Woolly Aphis, or **American Blight** is a pest that protects itself with a cotton-wool-like covering. The ordinary sprays are of no use. The best way to deal with this trouble is to apply methylated spirits with a stiff brush, working it in well.

Woodlice live in dark corners and under the staging. They feed at night on young shoots and the roots of plants.

---

* BHC stands for benzene-hexachloride. There are several proprietary brands, such as Sybol and Lindex.

Naphthalene will keep them away, but scooped out potatoes will trap them when they can be destroyed.

Diseases

Botrytis cinerea, is better known under the name *Grey Mould*, which is a good description of its appearance. The affected tissues turn black, soft and rotten. It is a difficult disease to get rid of, flourishing in close, damp, cool, conditions, particularly in winter and early spring. Strawberries, lettuces (especially winter sorts), tomatoes, melons and cucumbers are particularly susceptible.

Careless watering will encourage its development and ventilation does much to reduce the trouble. Burn all infected plants. Orthocide will check the disease, but on edible crops it is safer to dust frequently with flowers of sulphur.

Damping-off disease attacks tiny seedlings at ground level, causing them to turn brown and shrivel. It is a condition often encouraged by sowing seeds too thickly, and in too much heat, while badly drained soil adds to the condition. It can be *prevented* by watering the soil with Cheshunt Compound before sowing or pricking-out.

A very similar disease, which attacks older plants, is known as **Foot Rot.** Among the plants which are sometimes attacked by Foot Rot are calceolarias, carnations, petunias, pelargoniums and schizanthus. This disease cannot flourish under airy conditions, so that attention to ventilation is important, as is the provision of well drained soil, while watering needs to be carefully done, particularly in the early spring and from late autumn onwards. Here again, Cheshunt Compound solution applied instead of normal watering should keep Foot Rot in check.

Mildew is a white powdering that is liable to appear on many types of plants. Often it gains a hold on the undersides of the foliage, and if unchecked there, it will spread rapidly. The treatment is to spray or smoke with Karathane at the very first sign.

Much is heard about **virus diseases** and, although considerable research has been carried out, there is still a lot we do not know about them. They can certainly be spread by green fly, which is one reason for dealing with this pest in its early stages of attack.

Virus has many forms, and often shows as mottled foliage, sometimes the marks being quite attractive. On other occasions, the foliage become quite distorted and curiously marked. It must not be assumed all plants bearing marked foliage are suffering from virus disease.

Once it is certain plants are affected, they should be burned and not left lying about. After handling affected plants, wash the hands in a disinfectant solution. The growing of healthy stock and the maintenance of clean conditions in the greenhouse minimizes the risk of disease.

APPENDICES

Some Gardening Terms

Acid soil. Soil deficient in lime.

Alkaline soil. One containing lime.

Bracts. Rudimentary leaves at base of flowers.

Calyx. The cup of sepals holding the flower buds.

Crocks. Pieces of broken flower pots and similar material.

Disbud. To remove surplus buds or shoots.

Forcing. To hurry into growth by artificial means.

Harden-off. To accustom a plant gradually to a lower temperature.

Heel cutting. A side-shoot plucked from a main stem with a fragment of the bark or wood.

Heeling-in. A term used for temporary planting by making a shallow trench or hole and covering the roots.

Lateral. A shoot growing sideways from the main stem.

Loam. A mixture of clay, sand and humus.

New wood. The current season's growth.

Nodes or *joints.* The joints on a plant stem at which leaves appear.

Pinching-out. Removing a growing point of a plant, usually with the fingers.

Potting-on. Transferring to a larger pot.

Potting-up. Transplanting seedlings from boxes to pots.

Pricking-out. Moving seedlings from boxes or pans to other boxes at wider spacing.

Scape. A flower stem of bulbous plants arising from ground level and bearing no leaves.

Stopping. Same as pinching.

Whorl. A group of flowers or leaves arising in a circle from the same level on all sides of the stem.

Quantities Required

One bushel of compost will:

Pot about 100 plants in 3-in. pots and 50 plants in $4\frac{1}{2}$-in. pots.

Repot about 50 plants from 3-in. to $4\frac{1}{2}$-in. pots, and 20 plants from $4\frac{1}{2}$-in. into 7-in. pots.

Make about 60 large soil blocks, or 150 small soil blocks.

Fill (i) a rectangular box 22 in. × 10 in. × 10 in. deep; (ii) four two-gallon buckets; (iii) nine standard seed boxes 14 in. × $8\frac{1}{2}$ in. × 3 in. deep.

A standard seed box 14 in. × $8\frac{1}{2}$ in. will hold 40 plants in five rows of eight, $1\frac{3}{4}$ in. apart; 54 plants in six rows of nine, $1\frac{1}{2}$ in. apart; 60 plants in six rows of ten, $1\frac{1}{4}$ in. apart.

Composts

The John Innes Composts are suitable for all types of greenhouse work and do not require the use of fibrous loam (rotted turf) since the fibre is added in the form of peat. Any good soil can be used if it is neither too sandy nor too clayey and has a pH of 6·3, provided that it is first sterilized. Peat must be of the granulated moss or sedge type; the sand must be coarse river sand (not fine silver sand) with particles ranging from $\frac{1}{16}$ in. to $\frac{1}{8}$ in. The composts can be bought ready mixed but must be used within a month. Go to a first-class supplier; there is a lot of bogus stuff in some shops.

(N.B. – Soil dug from the garden, unsterilized and unmixed with other materials, should not be used in the greenhouse.)

J.I. Seed Compost: loam 2, peat 1, sand 1, parts by bulk; plus $1\frac{1}{2}$ oz. superphosphate, $\frac{3}{4}$ oz. ground chalk, per bushel.

J.I. Potting Compost No. 1 for the first potting: loam 7, peat 3, sand 2, parts by bulk; plus $\frac{1}{4}$ lb. J.I. Base, $\frac{3}{4}$ oz. ground chalk, per bushel.

J.I. Potting Compost No. 2 for the second and subsequent pottings of most plants: as above but double the quantities of J.I. Base and chalk.

J.I. Potting Compost No. 3 for chrysanthemums, cucumbers and tomatoes: as J.I. Potting No. 1, but treble the quantities of J.I. Base and chalk.

J.I. Base: 2 parts (by weight) hoof-and-horn meal $\frac{1}{8}$ in. grist (12 per cent nitrogen); 2 parts superphosphate (16 per cent phosphoric acid); 1 part sulphate of potash (48 per cent potash). It can be bought ready mixed.

Flower-Pot Sizes

Clay flower-pots are made in 'casts'. The smaller the pot, the more result from one cast. The pot size represents the number made from one cast.

Number	Inside diameter at top Ins.	Depth
60s Small	$2\frac{3}{4}$	3
60s Medium	3	$3\frac{1}{2}$
60s Large	$3\frac{1}{2}$	4
60s Long Tom	3	4
54s Small	4	$4\frac{1}{2}$
54s Long Tom	$3\frac{1}{2}$	$4\frac{1}{2}$
48s	$4\frac{3}{4}$	5
40s	$4\frac{1}{4}$	$5\frac{1}{2}$
32s	$6\frac{1}{4}$	6
28s	7	7
24s	$7\frac{1}{2}$	8
16s	$8\frac{1}{2}$	9
12s	10	10

Long Toms are rimless and deeper than ordinary pots. There are also the very small 'thimbles' and 'thumbs'.

Some Reliable Suppliers

The following is a selection of some of the leading suppliers of greenhouses, equipment, plants, seeds, bulbs, etc.

Pot-plants
C. S. Daniels Ltd., Wymondham, Norfolk.
Elm Garden Nurseries, Claygate, Surrey.

Thomas Butcher Ltd., Shirley, Croydon.
Thomas Rochford & Sons, Turnford Hall Nurseries, Brox-
bourne, Herts (especially for 'house plants').

Begonias and Gloxinias
Blackmore & Langdon, Bath, Somerset.

Pelargoniums
Anthony C. Ayton Ltd., Southborough, Tunbridge Wells.
Caledonian Nurseries, Maidstone Road, Rainham, Kent.

Bulbous Plants
Walter Blom & Son Ltd., Coombeland Nurseries, Leaves-
don, Watford.
G. B. Rawinsky, Primrose Hill Nursery, Haslemere, Surrey
(Lilies).
Wallace & Barr Ltd., Marden, Kent.
R. Wallace & Co. Ltd., Tunbridge Wells (Lilies).

Seedsmen
Thomas Butcher Ltd., Shirley, Croydon, Surrey.
Carter's Tested Seeds Ltd., Raynes Park, London, S.W.20.
Dobie & Son, Grosvenor Street, Chester.
Holtz Hausen, 14 High Cross Street, St Austell, Cornwall.
Sutton & Sons Ltd., Reading, Berks.
Thompson & Morgan Ltd., London Road, Ipswich.
Toogood & Sons Ltd., Southampton.
W. J. Unwin Ltd., Histon, Cambridge.

Saintpaulias
W. C. Wicks, Lambley, Notts.

Carnations
Allwood Bros. Ltd., Haywards Heath, Sussex.

Chrysanthemums
H. Woolman Ltd., Shirley, Birmingham.
Stuart Ogg, Swanley, Kent.
E. Riley, Alfreton Nurseries, Wooley Moor, Derbyshire.

Fruit
Thos. Rivers & Co. Ltd., Sawbridgeworth, Herts.
Laxton Bros. Ltd., Brampton, Huntingdonshire.

Shrubs and Climbing Plants
R. C. Notcutt Ltd., Woodbridge, Suffolk.
Hiller & Sons, Winchester.
Waterer, Sons & Crisp, Bagshot, Surrey.

Soils and Composts
Walter Uwins, Spring Lane, South Norwood, London, S.E.23.

Greenhouse equipment
Simplex Dairy Equipment Co. Ltd., Sawston, Cambs.
Macpenny's Mist Propagation, Bransgore, Christchurch, Hants.
Woodman & Sons Ltd., Pinner, Middlesex.

Greenhouse heaters (electric)
Roberts Electrical Co. Ltd., Humex House, 11/13, High Road, Byfleet, Surrey.

Paraffin heating
George H. Elt, Eltex Works, Worcester.
Aladdin Ltd., Greenford, Middlesex.
The Valor Co. Ltd., 50/52, New Cavendish Street, London, W.I.
F. J. Bryant, Fishponds, Bristol.

Greenhouses
Cambridge Glasshouse Co. Ltd., Comberton, Cambs.
Castos Ltd., Donnington, Telford, Shropshire.
Crittall Manufacturing Co. Ltd., Braintree, Essex.
Robert Hall & Co. Ltd., Paddock Wood, Kent.
V. & M. Hartley Ltd., Greenfield, Oldham, Lancs.
Messenger & Co. Ltd., Loughborough, Leics.
Oakworth Greenhouses, Telford, Shropshire.
Pratten & Co. Ltd., Midsomer Norton, Bath, Somerset.
W. Richardson & Co. Ltd., Darlington.
Robinsons of Winchester, Hants.
G. S. Strawson & Son, Horley, Surrey.
C. H. Whitehouse Ltd., Frant, Sussex.

INDEX